Presidents Time Line

Revised and Updated

Written by Ellen & Dick Sussman

Illustrated by Bron Smith

Teaching & Learning Company, a Lorenz company
P.O. Box 802
Dayton, OH 45401-0802
www.teachinglearning.com

D1361554

This book belongs to

_____

Cover design by Sara King

Photos obtained from the Photoduplication Service of the Library of Congress

ISBN No. 978-1-57310-394-7

Printing No. 987654321

Teaching & Learning Company, a Lorenz company
P.O. Box 802
Dayton, OH 45401-0802
www.teachinglearning.com

TLC10394

Table of Contents

★★

Dear Teacher or Parent,

As of 2009, 44 men have held the office of President of the United States. Beginning with George Washington, who took office in 1789, these men have been as individual as any other 42 men the world over. Some campaigned vigorously to become chief executive; others ended up in the Oval Office by sheer fate. Some achieved great successes during their term and left a memorable mark on the history of the United States. Others left no indelible marks; some were regarded by historians as failures.

Individually and collectively, the time line facts represent a reporting of historical, significant and fascinating information. William Henry Harrison has the unfortunate distinction of being the President serving the shortest term. Not wearing a coat on a freezing inauguration day in 1841, he gave a lengthy two-hour speech, led a parade back to the White House, caught a cold and died of pneumonia 31 days later. Grover Cleveland was the only President who served two separate terms; he was the 22nd and the 24th President. Franklin D. Roosevelt, the only President to be elected to four consecutive terms in office, served 12 years but didn't live to complete his last four-year term. After his long tenure, Congress passed the 22nd Amendment to the Constitution limiting a President's time in office. And rather than face impeachment, Richard Nixon resigned from office, becoming the only President in the history of the United States to do so.

Four presidents—William Henry Harrison, Zachary Taylor, Warren Harding and Franklin D. Roosevelt died while in office. Four Presidents—Abraham Lincoln, James Garfield, William McKinley and John Kennedy were assassinated while in office. Other Presidents have been victims of attempted assassinations.

President Kennedy's death in 1963 continued the extraordinary coincidence that between 1840 and 1960, every President elected in a year ending in "0" had died while in office.

> William Henry Harrison was elected in 1840.
> Abraham Lincoln was elected in 1860.
> James Abram Garfield was elected in 1880.
> William McKinley was elected in 1900.
> Warren Gamaliel Harding was elected in 1920.
> Franklin Delano Roosevelt was elected in 1940.
> John Fitzgerald Kennedy was elected in 1960.

Ronald Reagan, elected in 1980, broke this exceptional—but historically interesting—pattern.

In researching the lives of the 44 men who have served as our Presidents, it was especially moving to read about the high number of Presidents' children who didn't live to maturity. Without penicillin and antibiotics, sore throats, fevers and childhood illnesses were usually fatal. In the 1800s, the President's wives were often invalids by age 40 and were unable to serve as official First Ladies. In many instances, a President's sister or daughter served as White House hostess. Medically, we've come a long, long way.

We tend to view the White House as a mansion with every modern convenience and snap-your-finger services. But there was a time when all cooking in the White House was done over an open fire in the fireplace. In 1850, President Fillmore's wife Abigail had the first cooking stove installed. About three decades later, Rutherford B. Hayes was the first President to have a telephone and a typewriter in the White House. Along with the steps each President took to get to the White House, there's a historical trail of fascinating and intriguing facts about the man and his life—before, during and after his residence the executive mansion.

We've made many advances in many areas since George Washington took office in 1789, yet wars have been, and continue to be, a part of the history of the United States. Beginning with the American Revolution, we've endured the Civil War, the Spanish American War, World Wars I and II, the Korean Conflict, the Vietnam War, the Persian Gulf War and the war on terrorism. More now than ever, we aspire to a time when there will be peace between people of all nations. We hope one U.S. President will lead us in that direction.

Sincerely,

Ellen & Dick Sussman

P.S. Each time line details major events in a President's life. In between the years reported are many other events for children to read about and discover. The time line events are mentioned briefly and should serve as a springboard for further research, discovery, reporting and dramatization. Several sources were used in researching each President, and sometimes inconsistencies were discovered. *World Book Encyclopedia* was always the resource used for determining accuracy of facts.

TLC10394

George Washington
1ˢᵗ President of the United States

Term: 1789-1797
Party: Federalist

★ **1732:** George Washington was born on February 22 at Pope's Creek in Westmoreland County, Virginia.

★ **1752:** He inherited the rights to his family's Mount Vernon plantation upon the death of his brother Lawrence Washington.

★ **1759:** He married Martha Dandridge Custis, a wealthy widow with two young children.

★ **1776-1783:** As an Army General, Washington helped the 13 colonies win the Revolutionary War against the British. The colonists formed the American Continental Army and Congress unanimously selected Washington as commander in chief.

The soldiers were not well trained, and they lacked adequate food, weapons and uniforms. Their enemy, the British, were strong, well-equipped and disciplined. Washington organized his troops, motivated them, and against all odds was victorious. Now the colonists could focus on building a new nation.

★ **1787:** Washington presided over the Constitutional Convention in Philadelphia during which the U.S. Constitution was written.

★ **1789:** On April 14, at age 57, Washington was notified that he had been elected first President of the United States. He received the unanimous vote of the electors. He was inaugurated on April 30 in New York City, then the capital of the United States.

★ **1790:** On July 16, Washington signed plans Congress had approved for a U.S. capital on the Potomac.

The first national census began. It showed just under four million people in the United States.

★ **1791:** On December 15, the Bill of Rights became law. As the first 10 amendments to the Constitution, they guarantee basic liberties to Americans.

★ **1792:** Washington was unanimously re-elected by the electors as President for a second term. He was inaugurated in Philadelphia, Pennsylvania, which was the capital of the United States from 1790 to 1800. Rival national political parties began developing in the United States.

★ **1794:** Washington sent federal troops to crush an uprising by Pennsylvania farmers. This was the first test of federal power.

★ **1795:** Washington signed the unpopular Jay Treaty to maintain trade with Great Britain.

★ **1796:** On September 19, Washington published his farewell address refusing to run for a third term.

★ **1797:** Washington returned home to Mount Vernon in Fairfax County, Virginia.

★ **1799:** After riding his horse around his property for five hours in a snowstorm, Washington caught a cold and his throat became infected. He died at his home on December 14 at the age of 67.

★ **1802:** According to Washington's will, upon Martha's death all of Mount Vernon's slaves were freed.

After his death, the nation's capital was moved from Philadelphia to a location on the border of Virginia and Maryland near Washington's home. It was named Washington, District of Columbia, in his honor.

TLC10394

John Adams

2ⁿᵈ President of the United States

Term: 1797-1801
Party: Federalist

★★

★ **1735:** John Adams was born on October 30 in Braintree, Massachusetts. The Braintree of 1735 is now called Quincy.

★ **1751:** Although Adams was a poor student and did not like to read, he was accepted at Harvard College where he learned to enjoy school. Here he developed a gift for public speaking.

★ **1755:** After graduating from Harvard, he studied law with an attorney in Massachusetts.

★ **1758:** He began his own law practice and gradually built a good clientele in and around Boston.

★ **1764:** Adams married Abigail Quincy Smith of Boston, a woman who had strong views on law, politics and the rights of women.

★ **1774-1775:** Adams was elected as representative from Massachusetts to the First and Second Continental Congresses in Philadelphia. He joined Thomas Jefferson, Benjamin Franklin, and other delegates to draft the Declaration of Independence.

★ **1777:** He was selected as Minister to France.

★ **1780:** He was elected minister to the Netherlands.

★ **1785-1788:** Adams was appointed as the first U.S. minister to Great Britain, where he lived with Abigail.

★ **1789-1797:** Having received the second highest amount of electoral votes, Adams served two terms as Washington's Vice President, a job he described as "the most insignificant office . . ."

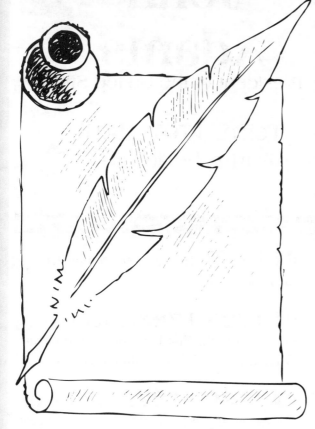

★ **1801:** The Adamses held their first and only New Year's reception at the White House. The Marine Band made its first official appearance and entertained.

★ **1818:** Abigail Adams died at age 74.

★ **1825:** At age 90, Adams lived to see his son John Quincy elected President.

★ **1826:** Adams died on July 4, the same day as Thomas Jefferson, and the 50th anniversary of the signing of the Declaration of Independence. Unusual for that time, he lived to be nearly 91.

★ **1796:** As Washington's Vice President, Adams was the natural choice to run for President when Washington rejected a third term in office. His opponent was Thomas Jefferson. Adams was elected and served one term. He was 61 when he was inaugurated.

★ **1798:** Under Adams, Congress organized the Department of the Navy.

★ **1800:** Washington, D.C., became the capital. The White House became the President's official home. President Adams was the first President to live in the White House. Without a water supply or staircases, the home was unfinished. He and Abigail moved in as construction continued.

Congress established the Library of Congress. Thomas Jefferson and Aaron Burr defeated Adams in his bid for re-election.

TLC10394

Thomas Jefferson

3rd President of the United States

Term: 1801-1809
Party: Democratic-Republican

★★★★★★★★★★★★★★★★★★★★★★★★★★★★★★★★★★★★★★★

⭐ **1743:** Thomas Jefferson was born on April 13 at Shadwell, the family plantation in Albemarle County, Virginia.

⭐ **1757:** When Jefferson was 14, his father died. This left him, the oldest son, as head of the family. He inherited the 2500-acre Shadwell plantation and at least 20 slaves.

⭐ **1760-1762:** After attending boarding school, Jefferson was educated at the College of William and Mary in Williamsburg, Virginia. After graduating, he began to study law privately.

⭐ **1767:** Jefferson began practicing law.

⭐ **1769:** Construction on Monticello began. It was the home that Jefferson designed and lived in most of his life.

⭐ **1772:** Jefferson married Martha Wayles Skelton.

⭐ **1774:** He retired from practicing law and inherited 11,000 acres of land and 135 slaves from his father-in-law.

⭐ **1775:** He was elected to the Second Continental Congress where he drafted the Declaration of Independence.

Parts of it were later changed by Benjamin Franklin, John Adams and others.

⭐ **1776:** Jefferson was elected to the Virginia House of Delegates where he worked to insure religious freedom for everyone.

He drafted the Virginia Statute of Religious Freedom which was passed by the state General Assembly.

⭐ **1779-1781:** Jefferson became the governor of Virginia. After the British invaded Virginia, he abdicated his office in 1781. The British overran Monticello and two of his other farms.

⭐ **1782:** His wife Martha died at age 34.

Declaration of Independence

⭐ **1783:** Jefferson was elected to Congress.

⭐ **1785:** Replacing Benjamin Franklin, Jefferson was appointed minister to France and returned to the United States four years later.

⭐ **1789:** He was appointed as the first Secretary of State under President George Washington and served four years.

⭐ **1796:** When John Adams was elected President, Jefferson was elected Vice President.

⭐ **1797-1801:** He served as Vice President.

⭐ **1800:** Jefferson was elected President of the United States at age 57.

⭐ **1801-1809:** He served two terms as President.

⭐ **1803:** The Louisiana Purchase took place. The vast territory west of the Mississippi doubled the size of the nation. This was Jefferson's greatest success during his first term as President.

⭐ **1804:** Jefferson sent Lewis and Clark to explore and map the newly acquired U.S. territory. They returned two years later. Jefferson was re-elected President. The 12th Amendment to the Constitution was passed providing that the President and Vice President be elected separately.

⭐ **1806:** As Jefferson was a widower, his daughters Martha and Mary sometimes filled in as White House hostesses. Martha, who was married to Thomas Mann Randolph, brought her children with her. Her seventh child, James Madison Randolph, was the first child born in the White House.

⭐ **1808:** Although he had been a slave owner, Jefferson passed a law prohibiting slave trade with Africa.

⭐ **1809:** At the end of his second term, Jefferson retired from elected office and public life. He returned to Monticello where he experimented with new crops and flowers, drew architectural sketches and read a lot.

⭐ **1819:** Jefferson founded the University of Virginia in Charlottesville and designed its buildings.

⭐ **1825:** The University of Virginia opened with 40 students.

⭐ **1826:** Fifty years after signing the Declaration of Independence, Jefferson died on July 4, at age 83. He wanted to be remembered for three main accomplishments: author of the Declaration of Independence, author of Virginia's Statute of Religious Freedom and Father of the University of Virginia. He ranked these accomplishments higher than being President of the United States.

TLC10394

James Madison

4th President of the United States

Term: 1809-1817
Party: Democratic-Republican

★★

⭐ **1751:** James Madison was born on March 16 in Port Conway, Virginia.

⭐ **1769:** He entered the College of New Jersey, now Princeton University.

⭐ **1771:** He graduated, completing the courses in two years instead of three.

⭐ **1774:** Madison entered politics when he was elected to the Committee of Safety in Orange County, Virginia.

⭐ **1776:** He served in Virginia's first legislative assembly where he met Thomas Jefferson.

⭐ **1779:** He was elected to the Continental Congress and served for four years.

⭐ **1787:** Madison represented Virginia at the Constitutional Convention. Although he was only 36 years old, he took a leading part. He helped write the Federalist Papers, urging ratification of the Constitution. In later years, he was called the "Father of the Constitution."

⭐ **1789:** He defeated James Monroe and was elected to the United States House of Representatives. During the time he served, he was largely responsible for drafting the first 10 amendments to the Constitution, the Bill of Rights.

⭐ **1794:** Madison married Dolley Payne Todd, a widow with a young son, on September 15. She quickly earned a reputation for being a fine hostess at political social events and often served as hostess at the White House for President Thomas Jefferson, a widower.

⭐ **1808:** Madison was elected President of the United States at age 57.

Dolley made official functions more elaborate. She was the first hostess to serve ice cream, a new treat, at the White House.

⭐ **1809-1817:** Madison served two terms. During his first term he inherited the problem of protecting American shipping from loss on the seas at the hands of Great Britain and France.

⭐ **1812:** Madison was re-elected President. Backed by many members of Congress, the United States went to war with Great Britain to protect freedom of the seas and the American shipping trade. This is known as the War of 1812.

⭐ **1814:** British troops staged a surprise raid on Washington and several public buildings, including the White House and the Capitol, were burned. President Madison was not at the White House during the raid, but his wife Dolley was. She was able to flee before the British arrived taking with her many state papers and Gilbert Stuart's portrait of George Washington. Francis Scott Key wrote "The Star-Spangled Banner" during the British attack on Baltimore. The Treaty of Ghent, signed by Great Britain and the United States ended the War of 1812. President and Mrs. Madison established a new residence in Washington in the Octagon House and later moved to another house nearby.

⭐ **1815-1817:** Madison's last two years as President were triumphant. The Era of Good Feeling began; it was a time of relative unity, peace and optimism in the United States. The Madisons retired to their family planation, Montpelier, in Virginia and remained active in national and world affairs.

⭐ **1826:** After the death of Thomas Jefferson, Madison became president of the University of Virginia.

⭐ **1829:** He served as a member of the Virginia Constitutional Convention.

⭐ **1836:** Madison died at Montpelier on June 28. Dolley returned to Washington where she lived until her death in 1849.

TLC10394

James Monroe

5th President of the United States

Term: 1817-1825
Party: Democratic-Republican

★ **1758:** James Monroe was born on April 28 on his father's tobacco farm in Westmoreland County, Virginia.

★ **1774-1776:** He attended the College of William and Mary in Williamsburg, Virginia. He left after two years to fight with the Third Virginia Infantry under General George Washington during the Revolutionary War.

★ **1780:** Monroe left the military and studied law under Thomas Jefferson, who was then governor of Virginia.

★ **1782:** He served on the Virginia Governor's Council.

★ **1783-1786:** He was elected to the Congress of the Confederation. Monroe married 17-year-old Elizabeth Kortright of New York City on February 16.

★ **1788:** Monroe was defeated by James Madison for a seat in the House of Representatives.

★ **1790:** He was selected by the Virginia legislature for a seat in the U.S. Senate.

★ **1793:** Monroe and his wife bought land in Charlottesville, Virginia, to be near their good friend, Thomas Jefferson. They built a home called Ash Lawn on 600 acres.

★ **1794:** Monroe was appointed minister to France.

★ **1799:** He was elected governor of Virginia.

★ **1803:** President Thomas Jefferson sent Monroe to Paris to help U.S. Minister to France Robert Livingston negotiate the purchase of New Orleans. When Monroe finally reached Paris, Napoleon of France had offered Livingston the entire Louisiana Territory. Without consulting with Jefferson, Livingston and Monroe arranged for the treaty.

Elizabeth Monroe

⭐ **1806:** President Jefferson named Monroe minister to Great Britain.

⭐ **1807:** Monroe was a reluctant candidate to succeed Jefferson as President, and was defeated by James Madison. He served in the Virginia Assembly.

⭐ **1811:** He was appointed Secretary of State by President Madison.

⭐ **1814:** When Secretary of War John Armstrong was forced to resign because of neglect of duty during the burning of Washington, D.C., President Madison asked Monroe to become Secretary of War.

⭐ **1816:** Monroe was elected President. The Monroes lived at another Washington residence for nine months while the White House was rebuilt after it was burned in the War of 1812. Era of Good Feelings began, and it was a period of peace and prosperity for the nation. The United States grew quickly. Spain sold its territory in the northwest and all its land east of the Mississippi to the U.S. Between 1816 and 1821 six new states became part of the nation.

⭐ **1818:** On New Year's Day, the Monroes held a public reception marking the reopening of the White House. After observing court etiquette on his trips to Europe, Monroe made the White House a formal place.

⭐ **1820:** Monroe was unopposed for re-election. The Monroes' daughter Maria, age 16, became the first Presidential daughter to be married in the White House. Congress approved the Missouri Compromise in March. Maine was admitted as a free state in 1820; Missouri was admitted as a slave state in 1821. However, slavery was banned from the rest of the Louisiana Purchase region north of the southern boundary of Missouri.

⭐ **1823:** Monroe proclaimed the historic Monroe Doctrine for which he is best remembered. In a message to Congress, Monroe warned European nations that the Western Hemisphere would no longer be subject to European colonization or interference. It remains a basic part of American foreign policy.

⭐ **1825:** Upon retiring from the presidency, Monroe and Elizabeth retired to Oak Hill, an estate near Leesburg, Virginia.

⭐ **1830:** Elizabeth Monroe died on September 23. Monroe moved in with his daughter Maria in New York City.

⭐ **1831:** At age 73, James Monroe died on July 4, the same date Thomas Jefferson and John Adams died five years before. He was the last of the Virginia dynasty of Presidents.

TLC10394

John Quincy Adams

6th President of the United States

Term: 1825-1829
Party: National-Republican

★ ★

☆ 1767: John Quincy Adams was born on July 11 in Braintree, Massachusetts. The Braintree of 1767 is now called Quincy. His father John Adams served as second President of the U.S.

☆ 1772-1778: As a child, John Quincy grew up listening to the sounds of the Revolutionary War around him.

☆ 1778: At age 11, young Adams sailed to France with his father on a ship named the *Boston* to France. His father's goal was to convince France to join the Revolutionary War on the side of the 13 colonies. En route, the *Boston* was chased by British warships, and survived an encounter with a pirate ship and a violent storm. Young Adams studied French, Greek and Latin while in Paris. He spent time with his father living in the Netherlands, Russia, Sweden, Denmark, and Germany. He began a lifelong habit of writing in a diary every day.

☆ 1780: At the age of 14, Adams was mature and smart enough to serve as secretary and interpreter to the American minister in Russia, and lived in St. Petersburg, for five years.

☆ 1785: He entered Harvard College and graduated two years later.

☆ 1790: Adams was practicing law and writing political essays, some of which were read by President George Washington.

☆ 1794: President Washington appointed Adams as minister to the Netherlands. On a diplomatic mission to London, he met Louisa Catherine Johnson, daughter of the American consul in London.

☆ 1797: John Quincy and Louisa were married on July 26, in London. They moved to Berlin, Germany, where they lived for four years.

☆ 1803-1808: Adams served in the U.S. Senate.

⭐ **1809:** He was appointed ambassador to Russia.

⭐ **1814-1815:** Adams helped negotiate the Treaty of Ghent with the British ending the War of 1812.

⭐ **1815:** He was named ambassador to Great Britain.

⭐ **1817:** Adams was appointed Secretary of State and served under President James Monroe. Adams was largely responsible for helping to develop the Monroe Doctrine.

⭐ **1824:** Four candidates—Andrew Jackson, William Crawford, Henry Clay and John Quincy Adams—ran for President. As no candidate won a majority of the votes, as provided by the U.S. Constitution, the House of Representatives chose John Quincy Adams.

⭐ **1825-1829:** John Quincy Adams was inaugurated on March 4, 1825, at age 58. He served one four-year term.

He and Congress did not get along well. Congress refused his requests to build a national university, weather stations, highways and other transportation systems.

⭐ **1828:** He ran for re-election but was overwhelmingly defeated by Andrew Jackson.

⭐ **1830:** The voters of Massachusetts elected Adams to the U.S. House of Representatives where he served for 17 years.

⭐ **1836:** Adams opposed the Gag Rules to keep petitions about slavery from being read on the floor of Congress. He believed this rule violated the constitutional right of free speech. He was the first congressman to assert the government's right to free slaves during war time.

⭐ **1848:** While still serving in the U.S. House of Representatives, Adams died on February 23 in Washington, D.C.

TLC10394

Andrew Jackson

7th President of the United States

Term: 1829-1837
Party: Democratic

⭐ **1767:** Andrew Jackson was born on March 15 in Waxhaw, South Carolina. His father died a few days before he was born.

⭐ **1780:** At the age of 13, Jackson left home with his 16-year-old brother Robert to become a courier in the Revolutionary War.

⭐ **1781:** The brothers were captured by the British and held prisoner. Andrew suffered cuts on his head and hands from an officer for not polishing the officer's boots as ordered. He had lifelong scars from the incident. At a military prison, Andrew and Robert came down with smallpox. Mrs. Jackson was able to obtain their freedom. Two days after reaching home, Robert died. Andrew's mother died, leaving him an orphan at 14.

⭐ **1784:** Jackson left Waxhaw and moved to North Carolina where he studied to become a lawyer.

⭐ **1788:** He moved to Nashville, Tennessee.

⭐ **1791:** Jackson was appointed attorney general by the western district of Tennessee. He met and married Rachel Donelson Robards.

⭐ **1794:** Jackson remarried Rachel when he learned her divorce had not been official.

⭐ **1796:** He was elected to the U.S. House of Representatives.

⭐ **1797:** He was elected to the U.S. Senate.

⭐ **1798:** Jackson resigned from the Senate and was elected judge of the State Supreme Court in Tennessee, an office he held for six years.

⭐ **1806:** A hot-tempered man who had been in several duels, Jackson killed a man in a pistol duel and suffered a serious wound.

⭐ **1813:** He refused to obey orders by Tennessee governor Willie Blount to demobilize his forces. Leading his men home through 500 miles of wilderness, he earned the nickname "Old Hickory" for being as tough as hickory.

⭐ **1814:** After the Creek Indians massacred several hundred settlers in the Mississippi Territory, Jackson took command of a volunteer force of 2000 men. He led the Indian women and children to safety before wiping out nearly 800 Creek braves.

⭐ **1815:** During the War of 1812, Jackson commanded the defense of New Orleans against the British. He won a great victory and became a national hero.

⭐ **1817:** President Monroe sent troops with Jackson to lead an expedition to Florida to crush Seminole raids on American settlements.

⭐ **1821:** Two years after the United States acquired Florida, Jackson became provisional governor of the new territory.

⭐ **1822:** The Tennessee legislature nominated Jackson to run for President in the election of 1824.

⭐ **1823:** Jackson was elected to the U.S. Senate for the second time.

⭐ **1824:** He was one of four candidates who ran for President. Although he won more popular and electoral votes than any other candidate, he did not have a majority of all votes cast. According to the U.S. Constitution, the House of Representatives chose the President. They selected John Quincy Adams.

⭐ **1828:** In a bitter campaign, Jackson defeated John Quincy Adams. Jackson's wife Rachel died in December, soon after he won the election.

JOHN QUINCY ADAMS

★ **1829:** He was inaugurated the seventh President in March. Thousands of well-wishers came to the White House, creating havoc by grabbing food, breaking china, starting fights, and being unruly.

★ **1830:** Jackson got Congress to pass a law authorizing him to create new Indian lands west of the Mississippi River and to transport Indians there. Jackson offered to open American ports to the British in exchange for equal trading rights in the West Indies. Britain accepted Jackson's offer.

★ **1832:** Jackson vetoed a bill to renew the charter of the Bank of the United States. South Carolina declared the federal tariff laws null and void. Jackson sent U.S. troops to the state. John C. Calhoun resigned as Vice President. For the first time, national political conventions chose

presidential candidates. Jackson was elected to serve a second term.

★ **1833:** He ordered Secretary of the Treasury Louis McLane to remove the government's deposits from the Bank of the United States and place them in state banks. McLane and his successor, William Duane, refused.

★ **1835:** Jackson was the first President to survive an assassination attempt. On January 30, there was an attempt on his life, but both of the assassin's guns misfired.

★ **1837:** At the final public reception at the Jackson White House on February 22, a 1400-pound wheel of cheddar cheese was the center of attention. The smell of cheese lingered for weeks. After seeing his friend Martin Van Buren sworn in as President, Jackson returned to his plantation, the Hermitage in Tennessee, where he continued his interest in national politics.

★ **1840:** He supported Van Buren's unsuccessful bid for re-election.

★ **1844:** He supported James K. Polk's successful campaign for President.

★ **1845:** At age 78, Jackson died on June 8. He was buried beside his wife in the garden of the Hermitage.

Martin Van Buren

8ᵗʰ President of the United States

Term: 1837-1841
Party: Democratic

★★

★ **1782:** Martin Van Buren was born on December 5 in the Dutch community of Kinderhook, New York. He was the first President born after the signing of the Declaration of Independence and the first President born a U.S. citizen.

★ **1796:** At the age of 14, he began to study law, and took an active part in a law case at age 15.

★ **1803:** Van Buren opened his own law office in Kinderhook.

★ **1807:** He was appointed as counselor to the state supreme court. On February 21 he married Hannah Hoes.

★ **1812:** Van Buren was elected to the New York Senate at age 30.

★ **1816:** Shortly after re-election to the Senate, he was appointed Attorney General of New York.

★ **1819:** Hannah Van Buren died at age 35, shortly after her fourth son's second birthday.

MARTIN VAN BUREN
Attorney at Law

TLC10394

★ **1821:** Van Buren was elected a U.S. Senator and became a leader in the fight against imprisonment for debt. He also tried to stop slave trade but was unsuccessful.

★ **1827:** He was re-elected to the Senate and became a supporter of Andrew Jackson for the presidency.

★ **1829:** Van Buren was appointed Secretary of State by newly elected President Andrew Jackson.

★ **1832:** Van Buren was elected Vice President of the United States.

★ **1836:** At age 54, he was elected eighth President of the United States, defeating William Henry Harrison. He moved into the White House with his four bachelor sons. He was the third President to live in the White House as a widower.

★ **1837:** Sixty-seven days after Van Buren took office, the first great depression in the United States began. Although Van Buren felt no responsibility, the people blamed him for the hard times. He became very unpopular. Dolley Madison introduced Van Buren's oldest son Abraham to a relative, Angelica Singleton. The two were married and Angelica Van Buren assumed the role of White House hostess.

★ **1840:** Van Buren ran for President and was defeated by William Henry Harrison.

★ **1841:** Van Buren retired to his 200-acre estate, Lindenwald, 18 miles south of Albany. He remained active in politics for more than 20 years.

★ **1848:** The antislavery Free Soil Party nominated Van Buren for President. He lost the election.

★ **1862:** At age 79, Van Buren died on July 24. He was buried beside his wife in Kinderhook, New York.

William Henry Harrison

9th President of the United States

Term: 1841
Party: Whig

★★

⭐ **1773:** William Henry Harrison was born on February 9 in Charles City County, Virginia. His father, Benjamin, was a signer of the Declaration of Independence.

⭐ **1787:** Until age 14, he was taught by tutors at his family's Berkeley plantation and then entered Hampden-Sydney College in Virginia. Without finishing his courses, he left to study medicine for two years in Richmond, Virginia, and Philadelphia.

⭐ **1791:** At age 18, Harrison joined the army as a junior officer fighting Indians on America's frontier.

⭐ **1794:** He was in the Battle of Fallen Timbers against the Shawnee Indians and later received an officer's commission from George Washington.

⭐ **1795:** While on leave from the army, he visited friends in Kentucky and met and fell in love with Anna Symmes. When Anna's father wouldn't approve their marriage, the couple eloped and were married on November 25. They eventually had 10 children. One son, John Scott, was the father of Benjamin Harrison who was elected 23rd President of the United States.

⭐ **1798:** Harrison resigned from the army and served as secretary of the Northwest Territory under President John Adams.

⭐ **1800:** When the Northwest Territory was divided into two parts, the Ohio and Indiana Territories, 27-year-old Harrison was appointed governor of the Indiana Territory.

⭐ **1811:** Harrison made military history when his outnumbered forces won the Battle of Tippecanoe against Tecumseh and the Shawnee Indians. He earned the nickname "Old Tippecanoe."

TLC10394

William Henry Harrison

⭐ **1812-1814:** President James Madison made Harrison a brigadier general in command of the Army of the Northwest. His troops won a brilliant victory over Indian and British forces in the Battle of the Thames in southern Ontario.

⭐ **1816:** Harrison was elected to the U.S. House of Representatives.

⭐ **1825:** He was elected to the United States Senate.

⭐ **1828:** Harrison was appointed U.S. minister to Colombia.

⭐ **1836:** He was one of three Whig candidates who ran against Democrat Martin Van Buren. Although he lost, Harrison made a decent showing, and the Whigs chose him to run again in 1840.

⭐ **1840:** With John Tyler of Virginia as his running mate, Harrison campaigned for President. The slogan "Tippecanoe and Tyler Too" became popular. Harrison won 234 of 294 electoral votes and was elected President.

⭐ **1841:** Harrison's wife was too ill to accompany him to Washington for the March inauguration, so he was accompanied by his widowed daughter-in-law Jane Irwin Harrison. At age 68, Harrison was the oldest President yet inaugurated. Not wearing a coat, hat, or gloves on the cold and windy day, he gave a two-hour inauguration speech, led a parade to the White House in freezing weather, and attended three formal balls that evening. The next morning he awoke with a severe cold and died one month later, on April 4 of pneumonia. He was the first President to die in office and his one month in office, made him the President with the shortest term on record. Anna Harrison received a pension of $25,000, the first pension to be given to a President's widow. She had not yet arrived at the White House when she received word her husband was dead. Harrison was buried in North Bend, Ohio. His wife lived until 1864.

Tippecanoe and Tyler Too!

John Tyler

10th President of the United States

Term: 1841-1845
Party: Democratic, Whig, None

★★★

★ **1790:** John Tyler was born on March 29. Like President William Henry Harrison, Tyler was born in Charles City County, Virginia.

★ **1800:** When he was 10 years old, he led his schoolmates in a rebellion against a teacher who was cruel to them.

★ **1807:** He graduated from William and Mary College at age 17.

★ **1809:** He was admitted to the Virginia bar.

★ **1811:** At age 21, Tyler was elected to the Virginia House of Delegates.

★ **1813:** In his teens, Tyler met Letitia Christian. They were married on his birthday, March 29.

★ **1817:** After serving five terms in the Virginia legislature, Tyler was elected to the U.S. House of Representatives.

★ **1821:** He ran for the U.S. Senate but lost.

★ **1825-1827:** He served as governor of Virginia and was elected to the Senate in 1827.

★ **1840:** Tyler was elected Vice President as a Whig although he opposed some Whig principles.

★ **1841:** When President Harrison died suddenly after only one month in office, Tyler became President. He was sworn in on April 6.

24

★ **1842:** Having suffered a stroke in the late 1830s, Letitia Tyler died. Tyler's daughter-in-law, Priscilla Cooper Tyler, served as White House hostess until the spring of 1844. Tyler brought an end to the Seminole War in Florida. His daughter Elizabeth became the second daughter of a President to be married in the White House.

★ **1843:** After Tyler vetoed many bills introduced by Whigs in Congress, impeachment resolutions were introduced against him, but were defeated.

★ **1844:** At age 54, Tyler married Julia Gardiner, the 24-year-old daughter of a friend, on June 26. He was the first President to be married while in office. The couple had seven children. Tyler had eight children from his first marriage, making him the only President to have 15 children. Julia renovated the White House and introduced a new dance called the polka.

★ **1845:** After vetoing many bills, Tyler was nicknamed "Old Veto." In March, Congress overrode a presidential veto for the first time. Tyler signed a resolution admitting Texas as a state. On his last day in office he signed a bill admitting Florida as a state. When the four-year term ended, Tyler did not run for President again. He and Julia moved to their retirement home in Virginia.

★ **1861:** When Virginia seceded from the Union, Tyler remained loyal to his native state. He was elected to the Confederate House of Representatives in November.

★ **1862:** At age 71, Tyler died on January 18 before taking his seat in the House. He is buried beside his second wife in Richmond, Virginia.

James Knox Polk

11th President of the United States

Term: 1845-1849
Party: Democratic

★★★

★ **1795:** James Knox Polk was born on November 2 in Mecklenburg County, North Carolina.

★ **1806:** When Polk was 11, his family moved to Tennessee. It took six weeks to make the 500-mile journey across the Blue Ridge Mountains.

★ **1812:** At age 17, Polk was sick, frail, and often in pain. A doctor discovered he had gallstones. If they were not removed, he would not get better. In a daring operation without anesthesia, the gallstones were removed. Polk became healthy and energetic.

★ **1818:** He graduated from the University of North Carolina at the head of his class. He returned home to Tennessee and studied law with Felix Grundy who introduced him to Andrew Jackson.

★ **1820:** Polk was admitted to the bar in Tennessee.

★ **1821:** He became chief clerk of the Tennessee Senate.

★ **1823:** Polk was elected to the Tennessee House of Representatives. He became a well-known leader in the state and was called "Young Hickory" because he was a loyal supporter of his close friend Andrew Jackson, "Old Hickory."

★ **1824:** On New Year's Day, Polk married Sarah Childress, who encouraged her husband's political career.

★ **1825:** Polk was elected to the U.S. House of Representatives where he served for 14 years.

★ **1835:** During Andrew Jackson's presidency, Polk became Speaker of the House of Representatives.

★ **1839:** He was elected governor of Tennessee and served one term.

TLC10394

JAMES KNOX POLK

★ **1849:** Worn out after four years of hard work, Polk and his wife left Washington in March and retired to their family home in Nashville, Tennessee. Three months later, on June 15, Polk died of cholera. He was 53.

★ **1891:** Sarah Polk lived for 42 years as a widow. She died on August 14. She was almost 88.

★ **1844:** Polk was the favorite to be Martin Van Buren's running mate in the presidential election. When Van Buren's opponents didn't support his nomination, Polk was selected as the Democratic candidate for President. He ran against Senator Henry Clay who had twice run for president and lost. Polk won the election by a narrow victory.

★ **1845:** At age 49, Polk was inaugurated on a rainy day in Washington. When he and his wife arrived at the inaugural ball, Polk ordered the dancing stopped because of his wife's religious beliefs. Sarah Polk became the first wife of a President to serve as his secretary.

★ **1846-1848:** War with Mexico gained much western territory for the United States, including Texas, Arizona, California, Colorado, Nevada, New Mexico, Utah, and Wyoming. In addition to fulfilling his four political promises, Polk kept his word that he would not seek re-election.

Zachary Taylor

12th President of the United States

Term: 1849-1850
Party: Whig

★★

★ **1784:** Zachary Taylor was born on November 24 in Orange County, Virginia. His family moved to Kentucky when he was a baby. His father fought in the Revolutionary War. His family was related to President James Madison and General Robert E. Lee.

★ **1808:** Taylor did not go to school but did learn to read and write. He joined the military and was made a first lieutenant.

★ **1810:** He was promoted to captain. On June 21 he married Margaret Mackall Smith, an orphaned daughter of a Maryland planter.

★ **1812:** Taylor was promoted to major for defending Fort Harrison in the Indiana Territory.

★ **1832:** He fought in the Black Hawk War in the areas that are present-day Wisconsin and Illinois and received the surrender of Chief Black Hawk.

★ **1837:** Taylor defeated the Seminole Indians at Lake Okeechobee, a victory that brought him the honorary rank of brigadier general.

★ **1840-1845:** The Taylors moved to Fort Smith, Arkansas; Fort Gibson, Oklahoma; and Fort Jesup, Louisiana.

★ **1846:** When Mexico threatened war with the United States over the annexation of Texas, President Polk sent Taylor to command troops in the disputed territory between Mexico and the U.S. Taylor defeated Mexican forces at Palo Alto in southern Texas and Resaca de la Palma in Monterey, Mexico. Congress declared war on Mexico on May 13. Taylor invaded Mexico and captured Matamoros and Monterey.

Zachary Taylor

TLC10394

★ **1847:** On February 22 and 23, Taylor's 5000-man army was attacked by approximately 18,000 Mexican troops in the Battle of Buena Vista. Although greatly outnumbered, Taylor's troops were victorious over the forces of Santa Anna. The victory made Taylor a national hero.

★ **1848:** The Whig Party believed it needed a national hero to win the presidential election. Although Taylor had no political experience, he accepted the nomination. His vice presidential running mate was Millard Fillmore of New York.

Although he had never voted, Taylor won the election. He was inaugurated on March 5 at the age of 65. Margaret did not want to leave her home in Louisiana and move to the White House, but in time did move. Their daughter Mary Elizabeth acted as official hostess.

Taylor's favorite horse, Whitney, who had carried him through many battles, came with him to the White House.

★ **1849-1850:** Although Taylor owned more than 100 slaves, he did not favor the extension of slavery to new states. Debates over slavery in Congress came close to bringing about a civil war. President Taylor opposed any type of compromise with slave states, but before the issue was settled, he was dead.

After attending a celebration near the Washington Monument on July 4, Taylor fell seriously ill and died five days later. He was 66 years old and had served 16 months as President.

He was buried in the family cemetery in Louisville, Kentucky. His horse Whitney followed his body in the funeral procession.

★ **1852:** Margaret died two years later and was buried beside her husband.

Millard Fillmore

13th President of the United States

Term: 1850-1853
Party: Whig

★★

★ **1800:** Millard Fillmore was born on January 7 in Locke, New York. His childhood was spent plowing hoeing, reaping and doing other hard chores on his parents' woodland farm.

★ **1814:** He served as apprentice to a clothmaker at age 14.

★ **1817:** He began to educate himself when a library opened in his town.

★ **1819-1822:** When an academy opened, he enrolled in the school.

For a time his teacher was 21-year-old Abigail Powers. Fillmore taught elementary school while he studied law with a judge.

★ **1823:** Fillmore opened a law office in East Aurora, New York.

★ **1826:** He married Abigail Powers on February 5.

★ **1828:** He was elected to the New York State House of Representatives. Fillmore was re-elected twice.

★ **1832:** He was elected to the U.S. House of Representatives as a Whig. He served from 1833 to 1835 and from 1837 to 1843.

★ **1844:** Fillmore ran for governor of New York. He was defeated, and returned to practicing law.

★ **1846:** He became the first chancellor of the University of Buffalo in New York State.

★ **1847:** He became Zachary Taylor's running mate for Vice President.

TLC10394

⟨ Millard Fillmore ⟩

★ **1848:** He was elected Vice President when Zachary Taylor was elected President.

★ **1850:** When Taylor died suddenly after only 16 months as President, Fillmore became President. He was sworn in on July 10 at age 50.

He strongly favored a compromise on slavery and immediately replaced Taylor's cabinet with men who agreed.

Congress passed laws that made up the Compromise of 1850 and Fillmore promptly signed them.

Abigail Fillmore arranged for the first cooking stove to be installed in the White House. She also began to build a White House library. Congress voted $250 to buy books.

★ **1851:** When the Library of Congress burned, Fillmore and his cabinet helped fight the blaze.

★ **1852:** Fillmore sent Commodore Matthew C. Perry on an expedition to Japan to open that country to world trade.

He was not nominated to run for re-election. Abigail died less than one month after he left office. She was buried in Washington, D.C. Fillmore returned to Buffalo, New York where he practiced law.

★ **1853:** His daughter Mary died of cholera at age 22.

★ **1856:** Fillmore ran again for President but was not elected.

★ **1858:** He married Caroline Carmichael McIntosh, a rich widow.

★ **1874:** At age 74, Fillmore died on March 8 following two strokes. He was buried in Buffalo, New York.

⟨ Commodore Perry ⟩

Franklin Pierce

14th President of the United States

Term: 1853-1857
Party: Democratic

⭐ **1804:** Franklin Pierce was born on November 23 in Hillsboro, New Hampshire. His father was a general in the Revolutionary War.

⭐ **1820:** After attending boarding school in New Hampshire as a child, Pierce entered Bowdoin College in Maine. He was active in literary, political and debating groups. Two of his classmates, Henry Wadsworth Longfellow and Nathaniel Hawthorne, became famous American writers.

⭐ **1824:** He graduated from Bowdoin College and began to study law under the governor of New Hampshire.

⭐ **1827:** He opened his own law office in Concord, New Hampshire.

⭐ **1829:** He was elected to the New Hampshire House of Representatives.

⭐ **1831:** He was re-elected and became Speaker of the House.

⭐ **1833:** Pierce was elected to the U.S. House of Representatives.

⭐ **1834:** He married Jane Means Appleton, the daughter of a former president of Bowdoin College.

⭐ **1837:** After serving two terms in the House, he was elected to the U.S. Senate and became the youngest senator.

⭐ **1842:** Ill, unhappy living in Washington, D.C., and saddened by the death of two of her three sons, Jane Pierce convinced her husband to resign from the Senate. They moved to Concord, New Hampshire, where Pierce practiced law.

⭐ **1846:** When the Mexican War began, President Polk made Pierce a U.S. Army colonel. He was later promoted to brigadier general.

Franklin Pierce

TLC10394

First Lady Jane Pierce

★ **1852:** As the issue of slavery continued to divide the northern states from the southern, Pierce was chosen as an ideal "compromise" presidential candidate to unite his political party and the U.S. He represented a northern state, New Hampshire, but supported the slave owners of the south. He won the election by a landslide.

★ **1853:** Two months before the inauguration, the Pierce's third and remaining son died in a train accident. Grieving the loss, Mrs. Pierce did not attend the inauguration and inaugural balls were canceled because the Pierces were in mourning.

Inaugurated at age 48, Pierce became the youngest President in history (up to that point). Once in office, he supported slave owners. However he didn't stop the north's increasing opposition to slavery.

Pierce negotiated the Gadsden Purchase from Mexico, allowing an important southern railroad route to the Pacific Coast to pass entirely through U.S. territory.

He was the first President to have a full-time bodyguard.

★ **1854:** Pierce approved the Kansas-Nebraska Act, which allowed the territories in the northern part of the Louisiana Purchase to choose whether or not to allow slavery.

The Senate approved a trade treaty with Japan.

The Republican Party was established by anti-slavery groups.

When three of Pierce's diplomats claimed the United States had the right to seize Cuba from Spain, the public reacted against Pierce.

★ **1856:** Pierce was not re-nominated by his party for President.

★ **1857:** After leaving the White House, President and Mrs. Pierce traveled widely in the United States and Europe.

★ **1863:** Jane Pierce died in Andover, Massachusetts, at age 57.

★ **1869:** Pierce criticized President Lincoln's leadership. He died in Concord, New Hampshire, on October 8. He was 64 years old.

James Buchanan

15th President of the United States

Term: 1857-1861
Party: Democratic

★ **1791:** James Buchanan was born on April 23 near Mercersburg, Pennsylvania.

★ **1807:** At 16, he entered Dickinson College in Pennsylvania. He got excellent grades but was expelled for raucous behavior. He was re-admitted and graduated two years later.

★ **1809-1812:** He studied law in Lancaster, Pennsylvania, and in 1812 opened his own law office.

★ **1814:** He served two terms in the Pennsylvania legislature.

★ **1819:** Buchanan met, fell in love with, and became engaged to Ann Caroline Coleman. When the couple had a misunderstanding, Ann left to visit a sister in Philadelphia. She died there. Grief-stricken, Buchanan never married.

★ **1821:** He delved into politics and was elected to the U.S. House of Representatives where he served for 10 years.

★ **1831-1833:** President Andrew Jackson appointed Buchanan ambassador to Russia, where he negotiated the first trade treaty between the United States and Russia.

★ **1834-1845:** He served in the United States Senate and as Secretary of State under President James Polk.

★ **1853:** He was Ambassador to Great Britain under President Pierce.

James Buchanan

34

John Brown

⭐ **1857:** In the Dred Scott case, the Supreme Court ruled that slaves and their descendants were property, not people.

⭐ **1859:** John Brown and a group of militant slavery abolitionists seized a supply of weapons in Harper's Ferry, Virginia, which they planned to use to help slaves win their freedom by fighting against their owners. Brown was captured and hanged.

⭐ **1860:** Buchanan was not considered for re-election by northern or southern Democrats.

The new Republican Party chose Abraham Lincoln, who was against slavery. The Democrats were divided and chose two opposing candidates—Vice President John Breckinridge, who was pro-slavery, and Senator Stephen Douglas, who believed that states should decide the slavery issue by themselves.

Abraham Lincoln won the election. Buchanan faced his gravest times during the period between Lincoln's election and inauguration. South Carolina seceded from the Union on December 20.

⭐ **1861:** On February 4, Buchanan met with representatives of six other slave states—Alabama, Georgia, Florida, Louisiana, Mississippi and Texas—to form the Confederate States of America.

He retired to his 37-room estate, Wheatland, in Lancaster, Pennsylvania. He continued to follow the events of the Civil War, and he wrote a book defending his policies.

⭐ **1868:** Buchanan died at Wheatland on June 1 at age 77.

⭐ **1856:** Because he had been in Great Britain and had taken no stand on the controversial Kansas-Nebraska Act, which allowed settlers to decide whether to allow or ban slavery, Buchanan became a popular choice for President. He won the election.

He was inaugurated at age 65. Since he had not married, his niece Harriet Lane served as hostess at the White House.

Buchanan was opposed to slavery and tried to steer a compromise course on the issue. He believed that the federal government had no right to tell slave states what laws they should live by; as states joined the Union, they should independently decide whether to allow slavery or not.

Abraham Lincoln

16th President of the United States

Term: 1861-1865
Party: Whig, Republican

★★★★★★★★★★★★★★★★★★★★★★★★★★★★★★★★★★★★

⭐ **1809:** Abraham Lincoln was born in a small log cabin in Hardin (now LaRue) County, Kentucky.

⭐ **1816:** The Lincoln family moved to Indiana. Lincoln's father bought land, built a log cabin, and farmed. Lincoln began to educate himself by going to school and reading the Bible and other books he could find.

⭐ **1818-1819:** Lincoln's mother Nancy died. One year later his father married Sarah Bush Johnston, a widow with three children. Lincoln became very close to his stepmother.

⭐ **1820-1828:** As Lincoln continued to educate himself, he worked at several jobs. He hired himself out as a farmhand and worked as a deckhand. Taking a cargo of farm produce to New Orleans once, he observed a slave auction.

⭐ **1830-1831:** Lincoln and his family moved 200 miles to Illinois.

He made his first political speech about improving navigation on a local river. He worked as a store clerk in a store in New Salem.

⭐ **1832:** He was a candidate for the Illinois General Assembly but did not win. The Black Hawk War broke out; Lincoln enlisted and served three months. He and a friend bought a store in New Salem.

⭐ **1834-1842:** At age 24, Lincoln was elected to the Illinois General Assembly as a member of the Whig Party. He served four consecutive two-year terms. He began to study law and met Stephen A. Douglas.

After earning his law license, he joined the law office of John Stuart in Springfield, Illinois. Stuart introduced Lincoln to Mary Todd. They later became engaged.

Lincoln made a trip by steamboat to Kentucky and saw 12 slaves chained together. He argued his first case before the Illinois Supreme Court and made his first public speech against slavery.

TLC10394

★ **1842:** On November 4, Lincoln married Mary Todd in Springfield.

★ **1843:** Lincoln was unsuccessful as the Whig candidate for U.S. Congress.

His first child, Robert Todd Lincoln, was born.

★ **1844:** He set up his own law practice and campaigned for Henry Clay in the presidential election.

★ **1846:** The Lincoln's second son, Edward Baker Lincoln, was born.

Lincoln was elected to the U.S. House of Representatives.

★ **1847:** He moved to Washington, D.C., with his wife and two sons and took his seat in Congress.

★ **1848:** Lincoln supported General Zachary Taylor for President.

★ **1849:** He left Washington and returned to Springfield to practice law.

★ **1850:** His four-year-old son Edward died after a two-month illness.

Lincoln repaid a $1000 debt and earned the nickname "Honest Abe." His wife gave birth to their third son, William Wallace.

★ **1853:** The Lincoln's fourth son, Thomas (Tad) was born.

★ **1856:** Lincoln joined the Republican Party, which believed in the abolition of slavery. At the first Republican convention, he received national attention when he won 110 votes for the vice-presidential nomination.

★ **1857:** He spoke out against the Dred Scott decision, in which the Supreme Court ruled slaves did not have the right to bring a case to court nor could they be citizens.

★ **1858:** Lincoln was nominated for the Senate and ran opposite Democrat Stephen A. Douglas. In a series of seven debates, Lincoln challenged Douglas arguing that slavery was wrong.

Although Douglas won the election, the debates made Lincoln a national figure.

Stephen A. Douglas

⭐ **1860:** In May, Lincoln was nominated by the Republican Party as a presidential candidate. He ran against northern Democrat Stephen A. Douglas and southern Democrat John C. Breckinridge.

On November 6, Abraham Lincoln was elected 16th President of the United States. He was the first Republican President.

On December 20, South Carolina seceded from the Union.

⭐ **1861:** Lincoln left Springfield, Illinois, by train for Washington, D.C. There had been a warning about an assassination attempt.

Alabama, Florida, Georgia, Louisiana, Mississippi and Texas seceded from the Union.

Lincoln was inaugurated on March 4 at age 52.

Six weeks after he became President, the Civil War began when the Confederates opened fire on Fort Sumter in Charleston, South Carolina. Lincoln issued a proclamation calling for 75,000 men to volunteer for the army.

On April 17, Virginia seceded from the Union. Within five weeks, Arkansas, North Carolina, and Tennessee seceded, forming an 11-state Confederacy.

In July, the Union suffered a defeat at Bull Run in Virginia.

⭐ **1862:** In February, the Lincolns' son Willie died at age 12 from a fever. Lincoln's wife was grief stricken and was unable to attend her son's funeral. It's said she never fully recovered. As Lincoln had been especially close to Willie, Lincoln, too, was emotionally overcome with grief and sadness.

Lincoln became especially close to his son Tad. His oldest son Robert was at school at Harvard College in Massachusetts.

In April, Congress abolished slavery in Washington, D.C.

Union forces won the Battle of Shiloh.

Congress approved the Homestead Act.

In September, Lincoln issued a preliminary Emancipation Proclamation, freeing all slaves in Confederate States.

Union forces won the Battle of Antietam in Maryland.

In December, the Union was defeated at Fredericksburg, Virginia, and lost over 12,000 men. The Confederates lost over 5000.

⭐ **1863:** On January 1, President Lincoln issued the final Emancipation Proclamation. Over three million slaves in territories held by Confederates were freed. Many fled to freedom, and about 200,000 helped the north win the war.

38

In March, the first draft law in the U.S. was passed. It gave the President authority to take men between the ages of 20 and 45 into the army.

In May, the Union was defeated at the Battle of Chancellorsville in Virginia. General Stonewall Jackson was killed. The Union lost 17,000; the Confederates 13,000.

In July, the Union won two victories—at Gettysburg, Pennsylvania, and Vicksburg, Mississippi.

Lincoln delivered the Gettysburg Address on November 19 and dedicated the Gettysburg battlefield as a national cemetery.

Free mail service began in 49 cities and soon spread throughout the country.

⭐ **1864:** Lincoln was nominated for President by a combination of Republicans and Democrats. In November, he was re-elected President, receiving 212 of 233 electoral votes and defeating Democrat George B. McClellan.

⭐ **1865:** Lincoln delivered his second inaugural address in Washington on March 4.

On April 9, General Robert E. Lee surrendered his Confederate army to General Ulysses S. Grant at Appomattox, Virginia, ending the Civil War.

On April 11, Lincoln made his last public speech, which focused on reconstruction of the Union. He spoke the famous words, "with malice toward none, with charity to all." The U.S. flag was raised over Fort Sumter.

On April 14, five days after the Civil War ended, President and Mrs. Lincoln went to Ford's Theater to see a play, *Our American Cousin*. Actor John Wilkes Booth shot President Lincoln in the head. Lincoln died the next morning. He was the first President to be assassinated. He was 56 years old.

On April 19, there was a funeral procession on Pennsylvania Avenue in Washington. Lincoln's body was then taken by funeral train to Springfield, Illinois, where he was laid to rest in Oak Ridge Cemetery on May 4.

On April 26, John Wilkes Booth was trapped in a barn and killed.

On December 6, the 13th Amendment to the U.S. Constitution was ratified, finally abolishing slavery.

⭐ **1871:** The Lincoln's son Thomas (Tad) died at age 18 from an illness.

⭐ **1882:** Mary Todd Lincoln died in July at age 63.

⭐ **1926:** Their son Robert Todd, born in 1843, was the only son to live to adulthood. He died at age 83.

Andrew Johnson
17th President of the United States

Term: 1865-1869
Party: Democratic, Unionist

⭐ **1808:** Andrew Johnson was born on December 29 in Raleigh, North Carolina. Neither of his parents could read or write.

⭐ **1821:** Johnson's father died when he was three years old. Although his mother remarried, his family lived in poverty. He had no formal schooling. At age 13, his mother made arrangements for him to be an apprentice with a tailor for six years. After two years, he ran away, although he had learned to cut, stitch, bind, and finish clothing. Throughout his life, he made his own suits.

⭐ **1823-1826:** Johnson opened a tailor shop in Carthage, North Carolina, then Laurens, South Carolina, and finally settled in Greenville, Tennessee, where his tailor shop did well. There he met Eliza McCardle.

⭐ **1827:** Johnson married Eliza on May 17. He was 19; she was 16. She taught him to read and do arithmetic, and she encouraged him to study. They had five children.

⭐ **1829:** With President Jackson as his role model, Johnson won his first election and became a municipal legislator of Greenville.

⭐ **1834:** He became mayor of Greenville.

⭐ **1835:** He was elected to the Tennessee House of Representatives.

⭐ **1843:** Johnson won the first of five terms to the U.S. House of Representatives.

⭐ **1853:** He was elected governor of Tennessee and favored laws to provide free education.

⭐ **1857:** Johnson returned to Washington as a U.S. Senator promoting the Homestead Act.

As the slavery issue became critical, he took a middle course. He believed the Constitution guaranteed the right to own slaves. However, he made it clear that his

TLC10394

Andrew Johnson

devotion to the Union was more important than his beliefs in slavery.

★ **1861:** When the Civil War began, Johnson, as a senator from Tennessee, was expected to join the Confederacy. As a strong supporter of the Union, he was the only southerner who remained in the U.S. Senate.

When Tennessee voted to secede, Johnson stood his ground and was seen as a traitor by many Tennessee citizens.

President Lincoln appointed Johnson military governor of Tennessee to give him military authority.

★ **1864:** A supporter of the Union, Johnson was chosen as Lincoln's running mate. Lincoln, a northern Republican, and Johnson, a southern Democrat, provided the right balance. They won by a large majority.

★ **1865:** On April 14, six weeks after his second inauguration, Lincoln was assassinated. At age 56 Johnson was sworn in as President the following morning. With the Civil War ended, he attempted to unite the country with his "Reconstruction" plan.

★ **1866-1867:** Johnson sparred with Congress over many bills. Congress overruled Johnson and passed several bills he had vetoed. Congress passed the 14th Amendment that included blacks as citizens. Johnson strongly objected to this.

During Johnson's term of office, Secretary of State William Seward convinced Congress to purchase Alaska from Russia. While many wondered why the U.S. would pay $7.2 million for land that was a frozen wasteland, it was seen as one of Johnson's great accomplishments.

★ **1868:** On February 24, the House of Representatives voted to impeach President Johnson because he had violated the Tenure of Office Act. Evidence against him was unclear. Conviction required 36 votes, or two-thirds majority. Johnson was found "not guilty" by one vote.

Johnson was the first President to face being removed from office by impeachment. As his last official act he proclaimed a complete pardon for all Southerners who had taken part in the Civil War. He was not re-nominated to run for President.

★ **1869:** The Johnsons returned to Tennessee without attending the inauguration of Ulysses S. Grant.

★ **1875:** Johnson later returned to Washington as a U.S. Senator from Tennessee, and became the only former President to serve as Senator. Many who had earlier voted to remove him from office applauded him.

Johnson did not live out his term in office. At age 66, he died on July 31 while visiting his daughter in Tennessee. He was buried in Greenville, Tennessee.

Ulysses Simpson Grant

18th President of the United States

Term: 1869-1877
Party: Republican

⭐ **1822:** Hiram Ulysses Grant was born in Point Pleasant, Ohio, on April 27. His parents always called him Ulysses or "Lyss." When a congressman was appointing Grant to West Point, he made a mistake and wrote Ulysses S. Grant. Grant never corrected the mistake.

⭐ **1829-1830:** While Grant went to school, he learned how to guide and control horses and became an excellent rider.

⭐ **1839:** When he was 17, Grant got an appointment to the U.S. Military Academy at West Point. There he joined cadets who, like him, became well-known during the Civil War. Fifty of his West Point classmates fought with or against him in the war.

⭐ **1843:** Grant graduated from West Point and was assigned to the Jefferson Barracks outside St. Louis, Missouri, as a second lieutenant.

⭐ **1844:** In Missouri, he met Julia Dent, the sister of a West Point cadet. The army sent Grant to Louisiana.

⭐ **1845-1848:** Grant was sent to Texas. He was in an area claimed by both the U.S. and Mexico when the Mexican War began. He took part in the capture of Mexico City and was praised and promoted for his skill and bravery.

When the war ended, he returned home. He and Julia were married on August 22.

⭐ **1849-1853:** Grant was stationed in New York and Michigan, where he lived with Julia. He was sent to Vancouver, in the Oregon Territory, but was unable to bring his family. He was promoted to captain and reassigned to California.

Ulysses S. Grant

TLC10394

★ **1854:** Because he missed his family so much, he began to drink alcohol. He resigned from the army and returned to his family in St. Louis, Missouri.

★ **1855-1860:** Grant had several jobs and business failures; for a time, he tried farming in Missouri. The Grants had two more children.

There was much hardship and poverty.

In 1859, he freed his only slave.

Grant went to work in his father's leather shop and moved to Galena, Illinois. His military career seemed to be over.

Supporters of Abraham Lincoln held a victory celebration at the shop where Grant impressed a Republican congressman.

★ **1861:** Grant helped organize companies of Illinois volunteers when the Civil War began and discovered his ability to lead. He led one outfit against Confederates in Missouri. Lincoln made Grant a brigadier general, and he became the north's most successful commander.

★ **1862:** At Fort Donelson, in Tennessee, Grant demanded the unconditional and immediate surrender of Confederate forces and became a national hero.

★ **1863:** He led Union troops to victory at Vicksburg, Mississippi.

★ **1864:** President Lincoln made Grant a lieutenant general and commander of all Union armies.

★ **1865:** Grant's troops faced severe losses in battle, but he faced the Army of Northern Virginia under the command of General Robert E. Lee, a fellow officer in the Mexican War. Grant attacked over and over. Lee surrendered to Grant on April 9 at Appomattox, Virginia, signifying the end of the Civil War.

★ **1868:** Southerners appreciated Grant's terms when General Lee surrendered. Grant became the Republican's choice for presidential candidate.

He won the election and was inaugurated on March 4 at age 46.

Grant admitted he had no political experience. He appointed friends, some relatives, and army officers to cabinet and government positions.

During his first term, from 1869 to 1873, Grant's administration worked to bring the North and South closer together. He tried to maintain the rights of southern blacks. He used federal troops to protect blacks from the Ku Klux Klan.

★ **1872:** Grant was easily re-elected for a second term. It wasn't long before corruption in his administration was publicized. Some whom Grant had appointed let him down by making poor decisions and taking bribes. While Grant was not personally involved, he was blamed.

★ **1873:** Several big banks in the East failed and financial panic swept the country. Bankers, manufacturers, and farmers were most affected.

★ **1874:** The Democrats won a large victory in congressional elections.

★ **1876:** In spite of a growing list of scandals, Republicans wanted to nominate Grant for a third term; he refused to run again.

★ **1877-1879:** After he left office, Grant and his family traveled to Europe and the Far East. When he returned home, his railroad investments did not earn interest income as the railroad fell on hard times. He went into a business venture with a brother. They began investing and losing whatever money he had.

★ **1881:** He moved to New York City.

★ **1884:** To earn an income, Grant began writing newspaper articles about his war experiences, focusing on the Civil War period. He also began to write his memoirs, and with American author Mark Twain as his publisher, his memoirs were a great success.

★ **1885:** Grant was dying of throat cancer. He moved to Saratoga, New York, and soon after finishing his memoirs, he died on July 23, at age 63. His military career had saved the Union.

★ **1902:** His wife Julia died. She was buried with her husband in Grant's Tomb on a bluff overlooking the Hudson River in New York City.

44

Rutherford Birchard Hayes
19th President of the United States

Term: 1877-1881
Party: Republican

★★★

★ **1822:** Rutherford B. Hayes was born on October 4 in Delaware, Ohio.

★ **1838:** A champion at spelling as a child, Hayes entered Kenyon College in Ohio and graduated four years later at the head of his class.

★ **1843-1845:** He entered Harvard Law School, graduated in two years, and was admitted to the bar, allowing him to practice law.

★ **1850-1852:** Hayes opened his own law office and received much attention in Ohio after saving clients from the death penalty in a criminal murder trial.

He met and married Lucy Ware Webb, the first wife of a President to graduate from college. She was outspoken for her time and supported the abolition of slavery and helping the poor.

★ **1861-1865:** Hayes joined the Army when the Civil War began. He distinguished himself in several battles, was wounded four times, and earned promotions during the war.

In 1864, while fighting in the Shenandoah Valley, Hayes was nominated to the U.S. House of Representatives. He refused to campaign because the outcome of the war was still uncertain. He won the election and took his seat in December, several months after the war ended.

★ **1866:** Hayes won re-election but resigned in July 1867, one month after he was nominated for governor of Ohio.

★ **1867-1872:** Hayes won the election to the first of three terms as governor. He had campaigned supporting an unpopular amendment, one that would give blacks the right to vote. He served two terms as governor. He then ran for Congress, but was defeated. For the next three years, Hayes worked in real estate.

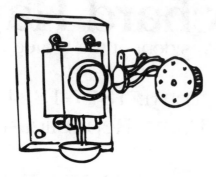

⭐ **1875:** He won a third term as governor of Ohio and worked to improve the state's civil service program. Hayes favored giving jobs to people based on merit and ability rather than friendship. During his terms as governor, he proved he was a capable leader and gained national attention.

⭐ **1876:** As President Grant's second term came to a close, the Republican Party was in conflict about selecting a candidate. Many supported Hayes as a compromise candidate. The results of the election were so close, that it had to be decided by a special committee of Congress. Hayes promised to remove troops from occupied southern states. As a result, the committee voted for Hayes, and he won by one vote.

⭐ **1877:** At age 54, Hayes was inaugurated on March 4. He was the first to be inaugurated in the White House rather than the Capitol. As he had promised, one of his first acts as President was to withdraw troops from southern states where they were still stationed.

⭐ **1877-1881:** Hayes had also promised to run only for one term so he could focus on civil service reform as he did when he was governor. As President, he appointed people to government jobs and posts based on their ability and merit, not because they were friends or had supported him for President.

Congress refused to act on Hayes' civil service reforms, but his work opened the door for future Presidents to make progress on this issue.

He was the first President to have a typewriter and a telephone in the White House.

In 1878, Mrs. Hayes began the Easter egg roll on the White House lawn, a tradition that lasts until this day. In the same year, Thomas Edison was invited to the White House to demonstrate his new invention, the phonograph.

As promised, Hayes left office after one term. He returned to his home, Spiegel Grove, near Fremont, Ohio. He worked to improve prison conditions, help veterans receive pensions, and provide education for all children, including African Americans.

⭐ **1889:** Mrs. Hayes died.

⭐ **1893:** After a brief illness, President Hayes died at his home on January 17 at the age of 71. He is remembered for ending the 12-year period of Reconstruction following the Civil War.

TLC10394

James Abram Garfield

20th President of the United States

Term: 1881-1881
Party: Republican

⭐ **1831:** James A. Garfield was born on November 19 in Orange, Ohio.

⭐ **1845:** During his teen years, Garfield worked as a farmer, Ohio Canal boatman, and carpenter.

⭐ **1851:** He attended Hiram College in Ohio for three years. He then studied at Williams College in Williamstown, Massachusetts, for two years.

⭐ **1856:** After Garfield graduated from Williams College, he returned to Ohio and was an ancient languages and literature professor. The next year, at age 26, he was chosen president of Hiram College. While teaching, he also studied to become a lawyer.

⭐ **1858:** Garfield married Lucretia Rudolph on November 11. She had been one of Garfield's students at Hiram College.

⭐ **1859:** He was elected to the Ohio State Senate as an anti-slavery candidate.

⭐ **1861:** When the Civil War began, Garfield enlisted and was made lieutenant colonel. He was made major general after riding under heavy fire to deliver a message to a general during the battle of Chickamauga.

⭐ **1862:** He became the youngest brigadier general in the Union Army. His distinguished service helped him win election to the U.S. House of Representatives. He was re-elected eight times.

⭐ **1876:** Garfield served on the commission that settled the disputed presidential election of Rutherford Hayes and Samuel Tilden.

James A. Garfield

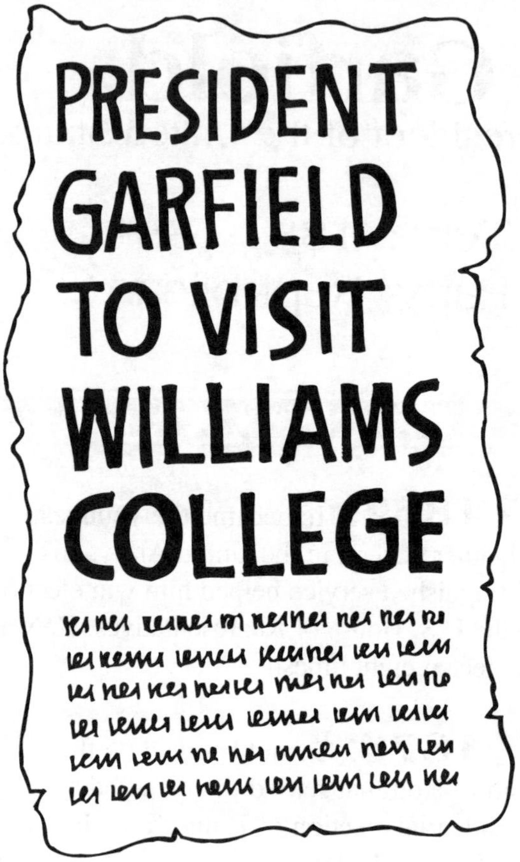

PRESIDENT GARFIELD TO VISIT WILLIAMS COLLEGE

[handwritten placeholder text]

⭐ **1880:** The Ohio legislature elected Garfield to the U.S. Senate. However, before he took his Senate seat, he became the "dark horse" or little-known Republican presidential candidate. One of the other candidates was President Ulysses S. Grant.

Garfield won, defeating his Democratic opponent Winfield Hancock.

⭐ **1881:** He was inaugurated at age 49 and moved into the White House with his wife and five children.

Once in office, he overturned former President Hayes' civil service improvements. To the disappointment of many, he rewarded his friends and supporters by giving them government jobs. Many workers who had been appointed by President Hayes due to their abilities lost their jobs.

In early July, Garfield planned a visit to Williams College in Massachusetts. He had planned to enroll two of his sons while attending his 25th class reunion.

On July 1, newspapers printed the President's plans to leave Washington, D.C., the following day from the Baltimore and Potomac Railroad Station.

On July 2, a man named Charles Guiteau, who had been turned down by Garfield for a government job, shot the President twice. One bullet grazed his arm. The other became lodged in Garfield's back. Without X-ray equipment, surgeons could not locate and remove the bullet.

Garfield was moved to a seaside cottage in Elberon, New Jersey. He died 11 weeks later, on September 19, from an infection related to the gunshot wounds. He was buried in Cleveland, Ohio. He had served just four months in office.

Vice President Chester A. Arthur became President. Guiteau, the assassin, was tried for murder. He was hanged in 1882.

YES, I'M THE PRESIDENT'S BROTHER·IN·LAW

48

Chester Alan Arthur

21ˢᵗ President of the United States

Term: 1881-1885
Party: Republican

⭐ **1829:** Chester A. Arthur was born in Fairfield, Vermont, on October 5.

⭐ **1844:** Chester was a good student who developed an early interest in politics. At age 14, Arthur supported Henry Clay, the Whig Party's candidate for President.

⭐ **1847:** He graduated from Union College in Schenectady, New York, and began to study law while he taught school.

⭐ **1854:** Arthur became a partner in a New York City law firm and earned a reputation for defending black people. He won a case defending a black woman who was forced to leave a streetcar in Brooklyn. The case ended racial segregation on public transportation in New York City.

He joined the Republican Party soon after it was formed.

⭐ **1859:** On October 25, he married Ellen Lewis Herndon.

⭐ **1861:** The governor of New York put Arthur in charge of outfitting the state militia in the Civil War.

⭐ **1862:** Arthur was made inspector general of the New York militia and then promoted to state quartermaster general. He was responsible for the troops food, transportation, lodging, and supplies.

⭐ **1865:** He became active in the New York City Republican Party.

⭐ **1871:** President Ulysses S. Grant appointed Arthur collector at the New York City Custom House. At that time, it was the largest single federal office in the United States with over 1000 employees.

Chester A. Arthur

⭐ **1872-1876:** Arthur used his position to help strengthen the Republican Party and gave good jobs to party supporters. He became head of the Republican state committee. All custom house employees had to contribute to the Republican campaign fund.

Arthur was at the heart of a corrupt and dishonest Republican organization.

⭐ **1877:** President Hayes appointed a commission to investigate the New York Custom House. Corruption and waste were discovered and President Hayes asked Arthur to resign. Arthur refused to resign until the Senate confirmed new appointees.

⭐ **1878-1879:** Hayes suspended Arthur. The Senate approved new officials in early 1879.

⭐ **1880:** Arthur's wife Ellen died of pneumonia on January 12 at age 42 leaving him with two young children.

The Republican Party split into two factions, the Half Breeds and the Stalwarts. The Half Breeds chose James Garfield as their presidential candidate and Chester Arthur as his running mate. Garfield won the election.

⭐ **1881:** When Garfield died in September, Arthur became the fourth Vice President to succeed to the presidency upon the death of the chief executive. Many people thought he would appoint supporters to government jobs, but he surprised the nation by changing his corrupt practices.

Arthur became President as a widower and had the White House redecorated before moving in. His sister served as hostess.

⭐ **1882:** Because Garfield was assassinated by a man who had been turned down for a government job, Arthur saw the need to create a better system for filling public jobs.

He vetoed a bill for improving U.S. waterways, but Congress passed the bill over his veto.

He also vetoed a bill to exclude Chinese as immigrants. When the bill was modified, Arthur signed it.

⭐ **1883:** Congress passed the Pendelton Civil Service Act, which set up the Civil Service Commission. It awarded jobs based on ability and merit as shown by examination. Arthur signed the bill on January 16.

⭐ **1884:** Arthur was ill with Bright's Disease, a kidney ailment, and discouraged friends from nominating him for re-election. He had run an honest administration and defended the rights of minorities, but Republican leaders were not behind him.

⭐ **1885-1886:** After leaving the office of President, Arthur returned to live in New York City as a lawyer. His health worsened. He died on November 18, 1886, at age 57. He was buried beside his wife in Albany, New York.

Grover Cleveland

22nd & 24th President of the United States

1st Term: 1885-1889
2nd Term: 1893-1897
Party: Democratic

★★

⭐ **1837:** Stephen Grover Cleveland was born on March 18 in Caldwell, New Jersey. When he was a young boy he dropped "Stephen" from his name.

⭐ **1855:** Cleveland and a friend headed west because they had heard there were good job opportunities. He got as far as Buffalo, New York, where his uncle lived. His uncle offered him a job and arranged for him to study and be a law clerk with a local law firm.

⭐ **1859-1873:** He held a variety of minor political offices, and was elected sheriff of Erie County, where he served for three years.

Cleveland worked with two law partners, and then opened his own office.

⭐ **1881:** Buffalo was one of many cities with corrupt leaders. Cleveland had shown he was honest and hardworking. Hoping for reform, Democratic leaders chose him to run for mayor. He stopped the corruption and vetoed measures that wasted city funds. His rise in politics began.

⭐ **1882:** Cleveland quickly gained a reputation as an honest politician and was nominated for Democratic governor of New York. He won by a landslide.

⭐ **1884:** His good and honest reputation made him known nationally, and he was nominated by the Democrats to run for President. James Blaine, his Republican opponent, had a reputation linked to corrupt government.

Cleveland won and became the first Democratic President since before the Civil War.

Grover Cleveland

The Interstate Commerce Act of 1887 was passed allowing the federal government to regulate interstate railroads.

⭐ **1888:** High tariffs had been in place since the Civil War to raise money for the government. Cleveland tried to remove these tariffs because they caused high prices for many goods. His presidential opponent, Benjamin Harrison, favored keeping the tariffs.

Cleveland won the majority of the popular vote, but Harrison won the electoral votes and defeated Cleveland.

⭐ **1889-1892:** Cleveland moved to New York City and practiced law.

⭐ **1892:** Americans wanted Cleveland back in office. He was once again nominated by the Democratic Party. He won and became the only U.S. President to serve two terms that did not directly follow each other. He faced an economic depression and high unemployment as banks, factories, and mills closed.

⭐ **1894:** Cleveland ordered federal troops to Illinois to break the American Railway Union-Pullman strike. He said strikers were interfering with the delivery of the U.S. mail.

⭐ **1896:** Cleveland was not re-nominated. He and his wife settled in Princeton, New Jersey, where he became a faculty member at Princeton University.

⭐ **1908:** After a three-month illness, Cleveland died on June 24 at age 71.

⭐ **1913:** Five years after Cleveland's death, Mrs. Cleveland married Thomas J. Preston, Jr., a Princeton professor.

⭐ **1885-1889:** He was inaugurated at age 47. Although President Arthur had begun a Civil Service program, Cleveland was besieged by many Democratic supporters for jobs. He tried to be fair by keeping Republicans who had proven their ability at their government jobs and appointing southerners to federal and cabinet positions.

Government tariffs on imported goods were a growing issue.

Cleveland married Frances Folsom, the daughter of his Buffalo law partner, on June 2, 1886. At 21, she was the youngest First Lady; the President was 49. He was the only President to be married in the White House.

Cleveland unveiled the Statue of Liberty on October 28, 1886.

Benjamin Harrison

23rd President of the United States

Term: 1889-1893
Party: Republican

★ **1833:** Benjamin Harrison was born on August 20 in North Bend, Ohio. He was named for his great-grandfather, a signer of the Declaration of Independence. His grandfather, William Henry Harrison, was the ninth President of the United States, and his father was an Ohio congressman. It can definitely be said that politics was in Harrison's blood.

★ **1852:** He spent his childhood on his grandfather's farm, where his father built a log schoolhouse and had a tutor for his children. Harrison graduated from Miami University in Ohio.

★ **1853:** After studying law in Cincinnati, Harrison married Caroline Lavinia Scott on October 20. She was the daughter of his former chemistry and physics teacher.

★ **1854:** They settled in Indianapolis, Indiana. Harrison was admitted to the bar, and he opened a law practice. Except for the time he served in the Civil War, Harrison practiced business law for the next 26 years. He also became involved in politics.

★ **1857:** Harrison became city attorney of Indianapolis.

★ **1858:** He became secretary of the Republican state central committee.

★ **1860:** He was elected reporter of the Indiana state supreme court and was re-elected twice.

★ **1862-1864:** The governor of Indiana requested that Harrison recruit and command a regiment of volunteers in the Civil War. He marched into Georgia with General Sherman, and before the end of the war, he was a brigadier general.

★ **1876:** Harrison ran unsuccessfully for governor of Indiana.

Benjamin Harrison

Although Harrison didn't win the popular vote, he did win the electoral vote and the election.

⭐ **1889:** Harrison was inaugurated at age 55. Life in the White House was photographed for the first time.

There was a Republican majority in the U.S. Senate and House of Representatives during Harrison's first two years. Many of his programs were passed.

Harrison's election marked the beginning of a connection between the Republican Party and big business.

⭐ **1890:** Harrison kept his campaign promise to extend civil service, and 11,000 more jobs were covered.

The four most important laws of Harrison's administration were passed. They included the Sherman Antitrust Act, the Sherman Silver Purchase Act, the McKinley Tariff, Act and the Dependent Pension Bill.

⭐ **1879:** He was appointed by President Rutherford Hayes to the Mississippi River Commission and served for two years.

⭐ **1881:** Harrison declined a post in President James Garfield's cabinet because he had been elected to the U.S. Senate.

⭐ **1888:** Because of his excellent war record, popularity with veterans, and his promise to keep high tariffs on imported goods, the Republican Party nominated Harrison to run for President. His opponent was President Grover Cleveland, who was running for a second term.

DING DONG

TLC10394

"I pledge
allegiance
to my
flag . . ."

★ **1891:** Electric lights and bells were installed in the White House.

★ **1892:** During his term, the U.S. Navy was expanded in the Atlantic and Pacific Oceans, and six states were admitted to the Union.

Harrison also increased respect for the U.S. flag. He ordered the flag flown above the White House and other government buildings and urged it be flown over every school in the nation.

The Republicans nominated Harrison to run for a second term. His opponent was the President who preceded him, Grover Cleveland. However, there were farmers unhappy with falling farm prices, angry factory workers charging federal interference, and those who opposed high tariffs and the McKinley Tariff Act. Cleveland defeated Harrison.

On October 25, two weeks before the election, Mrs. Harrison died.

Harrison returned to Indianapolis to practice law.

★ **1896:** Harrison remarried. His new wife was his first wife's widowed niece who had helped nurse Mrs. Harrison during her illness.

★ **1897:** He wrote a book titled *This Country of Ours* about the federal government.

★ **1899:** He represented Venezuela in a South American boundary dispute with Great Britain.

★ **1901:** Harrison died in his home on March 13 and was buried in Indianapolis.

This COUNTRY of OURS by Benjamin Harrison

William McKinley
25th President of the United States

Term: 1897-1901
Party: Republican

⭐ **1843:** William McKinley was born on January 29 in Niles, Ohio.

⭐ **1861:** When the Civil War broke out, McKinley was the first man in his hometown to volunteer for the Union Army. His bravery under fire earned him the rank of brevet major by the end of the war.

⭐ **1866-1867:** He studied law in Albany, New York, was admitted to the bar and began practicing law in Canton, Ohio.

⭐ **1871:** McKinley married Ida Saxton on January 25.

⭐ **1876-1890:** He was elected to the U.S. House of Representatives and served for 15 years. He supported high tariffs, and the McKinley Tariff Bill was passed in 1890. He lost his seat in Congress when anti-tariff Democrats won control of the House.

⭐ **1891-1893:** McKinley was elected governor of Ohio and was re-elected two years later. During his term, he improved the state's canals, roads, and public institutions and became a well-known national political name.

⭐ **1896:** He was nominated by Republicans to run for President. His Democratic opponent was William Jennings Bryan. While Bryan campaigned by train and traveled 20,000 miles, McKinley stayed in Ohio and conducted a "front porch" campaign. McKinley won both the popular vote and the electoral votes.

William McKinley

TLC10394

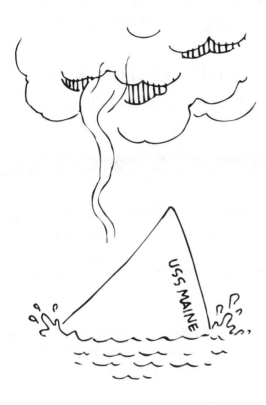

1897: McKinley was inaugurated at age 54. His wife was not in good health when she became First Lady but still attended many White House functions.

Cuba had been revolting against Spanish rule for two years. When McKinley took office, he tried to remain neutral.

1898: The U.S.S. *Maine* blew up and sank in Havana harbor on February 15. McKinley blamed Spain. On April 11, after his war message to Congress, America became involved in the Spanish-American War.

The war lasted only 113 days before Spain was defeated. It showed the United States to be a world power. By December the U.S. had signed a peace treaty with Spain. Hawaii, Guam, Puerto Rico, and the Philippines became American possessions.

1900: Winning the war and prosperity in the U.S. brought McKinley easy re-election. Governor Theodore Roosevelt of New York became his running mate. Once again McKinley's Democratic opponent was William Jennings Bryan, and once again McKinley defeated Bryan.

1901: McKinley changed his high tariff policy. He favored commercial treaties between nations. He felt this would help U.S. trade. He explained his new policy in a speech at the Pan American Exposition in Buffalo, New York, on September 5.

A day after giving the speech, McKinley attended a public reception. An assassin, Leon Czolgosz, shot him twice. President McKinley died eight days later, on September 14. Theodore Roosevelt took the oath of office and became the 26th President.

1907: Ida McKinley never returned to the White House after her husband was assassinated. She lived in Canton, Ohio, until her death. She and McKinley are laid to rest in Canton at the McKinley National Memorial, one of the nation's most impressive presidential memorials and burial sites.

Theodore Roosevelt

26th President of the United States

Term: 1901-1909
Party: Republican

★★★★★★★★★★★★★★★★★★★★★★★★★★★★★★★★★★★★

★ **1858:** Theodore Roosevelt was born on October 27 in New York City. As a child, he was frail, nearsighted, and had asthma. As he grew up, he exercised, became strong, and enjoyed outdo or activities.

★ **1880:** Roosevelt graduated with highest honors from Harvard University. On his birthday, he married Alice Hathaway Lee.

★ **1881:** At age 23, Roosevelt was elected to the New York state assembly. He was re-elected in 1882 and 1883.

★ **1884:** On February 14, there were two tragedies in Roosevelt's personal life. Two days after giving birth to their daughter, his wife died. On the same night, and in the same house, as his mother died. After their deaths, he left politics and went to a cattle ranch he owned in the Dakota territory. There he lived the life of a rancher and writer for two years.

★ **1886:** Severe snowstorms in the winter of 1885-1886 destroyed most of Roosevelt's cattle. He returned to New York City and re-entered politics. He ran for mayor of New York but was defeated.

He married Edith Kermit Carow, a childhood friend.

★ **1889-1895:** Newly elected President Benjamin Harrison appointed Roosevelt as civil service commissioner. Roosevelt established tests for some civil service jobs.

In 1895, he became the police commissioner of New York City and worked to stop dishonesty in the police force.

★ **1897:** President McKinley appointed Roosevelt assistant secretary of the Navy. In this post Roosevelt worked to strengthen the Navy.

When America went to war with Spain, Roosevelt recruited and commanded hundreds of cowboys from the west and former college athlete friends from the east for the First Volunteer Cavalry Regiment. They became known as the Rough Riders.

TLC10394

★ **1898:** As part of an American attack against fortified hills in Santiago, Cuba, Roosevelt led the Rough Riders in a charge up Kettle Hill. They became national heroes for this victory.

Roosevelt was elected governor of New York. Conservative New York Republicans nominated him as McKinley's Vice President. They didn't like his policies and wanted him to leave New York.

McKinley was re-elected, and Roosevelt became Vice President.

★ **1901:** When President McKinley was assassinated at the beginning of his second term, Roosevelt became the youngest President ever at age 42. He took the oath of office on September 14.

As President, he kept all of McKinley's cabinet members.

★ **1901-1905:** During his first term, Roosevelt worked to limit the power of big business. The Department of Justice won court orders to break up big business monopolies, which would increase competition in business and make prices lower.

Roosevelt created the Department of Commerce and Labor.

On a hunting trip on the Louisiana-Mississippi border, Roosevelt refused to shoot a bear cub. This event soon led to the manufacture of stuffed toy bears called "Teddy bears."

Roosevelt persuaded Congress to approve building 10 battleships and four armored cruisers to strengthen the U.S. Navy.

The U.S. signed a treaty with Panama that led to the construction of the Panama Canal to connect the Atlantic and Pacific Oceans. In 1906, Roosevelt visited Panama and became the first President to visit a foreign country while in office.

Roosevelt was the first President to make important achievements in conservation. He added 150 million acres to the national forests, established the U.S. Forest Service, and set up five new national parks. He worked to preserve wildlife and named 18 sites as national monuments.

Roosevelt was re-elected to a second term in 1904.

★ **1905-1909:** He acted as mediator in peace talks that helped end the Russo-Japanese War.

In 1906 he became the first American to win a Nobel Prize when he received the Nobel Peace Prize for his accomplishments in ending the Russo-Japanese War.

Roosevelt negotiated a "Gentlemen's Agreement" with Japan to stop the emigration of Japanese to the United States.

Congress passed the Meat Inspection Act and the Pure Food and Drugs Act in 1906.

In 1907, Roosevelt sent 16 new battleships on a 14-month goodwill tour of the world to display America's naval power.

In 1907, the stock market slumped. Prosperity returned in 1909.

In 1908, Roosevelt kept his pledge not to seek re-election. He named William Taft, his secretary of war, to succeed him. Most Republicans supported Taft for President and he won the election.

★ **1909-1910:** Upon leaving office, Roosevelt spent one year big game hunting in Africa. When he returned, he learned the Republicans were displeased with Taft as President.

★ **1912:** Roosevelt decided to run for another term. When two divisions of the Republican Party didn't support him, he and his followers formed the Progressive Party. Roosevelt was defeated, and Democratic candidate Woodrow Wilson won the election.

★ **1914:** Roosevelt disagreed with President Wilson about becoming involved in World War I with Germany.

On October 14, John Schrank tried to assassinate Roosevelt in Milwaukee. Roosevelt recovered from the gunshot wound.

After exploring the Brazilian jungle, he contracted a form of jungle fever. It left him weak and ill for several years.

★ **1918:** His son Quentin, an aviator serving in World War I, was killed in action in France at age 21.

★ **1919:** On January 6, Roosevelt died suddenly at age 60. He was buried near his home in Oyster Bay, New York. His wife Edith died in 1948 and was buried beside him.

Three historic sites honor Theodore Roosevelt's memory. He is one of four Presidents whose faces are carved on Mount Rushmore in South Dakota.

TLC10394

William Howard Taft

27th President of the United States

Term: 1909-1913
Party: Republican

★★

⭐ **1857:** William Howard Taft was born on September 15 in Cincinnati, Ohio.

⭐ **1878:** He graduated second in his class from Yale University.

⭐ **1880:** After studying law at Cincinnati Law School, Taft received his law degree and was admitted to the Ohio bar.

⭐ **1882:** President Chester Arthur appointed Taft collector of internal revenue for the first district in Cincinnati. He resigned after a year because he did not want to fire good workers to make room for Republican supporters. When he left, he formed a law partnership.

⭐ **1886:** Taft married Helen (Nellie) Herron on June 19. Her father had been a law partner of President Rutherford B. Hayes.

⭐ **1887-1888:** In 1887, the governor of Ohio appointed Taft to fill a vacancy on the Cincinnati Supreme Court. In 1888 voters elected him to the court for a five-year term.

⭐ **1889-1897:** The Tafts had three children. As adults one became a U.S. senator from Ohio, one served as a history professor and dean of Bryn Mawr College in Pennsylvania, and one became a lawyer and mayor of Cincinnati.

In 1890, Taft resigned from the Cincinnati Supreme Court to accept an appointment by President Benjamin Harrison as solicitor general of the United States. In his first year, Taft won 15 of 18 government cases he presented before the U.S. Supreme Court.

⭐ **1892:** President Harrison appointed Taft judge of the new federal Circuit Court of Appeals. Taft held the position for eight years.

⭐ **1896:** At the same time, Taft served as dean of the University of Cincinnati Law School until 1900.

⭐ **1898:** The United States gained possession of the Philippines.

⭐ **1901:** President William McKinley named Taft as first civil governor of the Philippines. Taft built roads and harbors, established schools and worked to improve and bring peace to the islands.

⭐ **1904:** He became secretary of war in President Theodore Roosevelt's cabinet. Taft's department oversaw the construction of the Panama Canal and set up the government in the Canal Zone.

Taft assisted President Roosevelt in negotiating a treaty which ended the Russo-Japanese War.

William Howard Taft

Nellie Taft had 80 Japanese cherry trees planted along the banks of the Potomac River. The mayor of Tokyo later shipped 3000 more cherry trees to Mrs. Taft as a gift from his city.

During Taft's first year in office, his wife had a stroke.

⭐ **1909-1913:** Taft supported a federal income tax amendment. In 1913, the 16th Amendment gave Congress the power to levy income taxes.

Congress established the Postal Savings Bank, the parcel post system, and the Department of Labor.

Arizona and New Mexico became the 47th and 48th states.

⭐ **1908:** Roosevelt announced he would not seek a third term and recommended Taft to succeed him. Initially Taft objected because his dream was to be a U.S. Supreme Court judge. His wife and family convinced him to run for President.

With Roosevelt's support, Taft won in a landslide. His opponent was William Jennings Bryan, who lost his third bid for President.

⭐ **1909:** Taft was inaugurated in March at age 51. A winter blizzard welcomed him as President.

Taft began his term with a divided Republican Party. He carried on Roosevelt's work against powerful companies while he supported workers' rights.

62

The Taft administration began more court cases to break up big business monopolies than Roosevelt's administration had.

Taft ran for re-election but was badly defeated by Democrat Woodrow Wilson.

Taft is credited with starting the tradition of the President throwing out the first pitch of the baseball season.

★ **1913:** Upon leaving office, President Taft became a professor of constitutional law at his alma mater, Yale University.

He was elected president of the American Bar Association.

★ **1914-1918:** President Woodrow Wilson appointed Taft to the National War Labor Board during World War I.

★ **1921:** Taft's dream of serving on the Supreme Court came true when President Warren G. Harding appointed him Chief Justice of the United States Supreme Court. He was the only man who served first as President, then as chief justice.

★ **1930:** Poor health, mostly due to heart trouble, forced Taft to retire on February 3. For most of his adult life he weighed over 300 pounds and was the largest President in history.

He died on March 8 at age 72 and was buried in Arlington National Cemetery.

Woodrow Wilson

28th President of the United States

Term: 1913-1921
Party: Democratic

★★

★ **1856:** Thomas Woodrow Wilson was born on December 29 in Staunton, Virginia. Some books may note his birth date as December 28, as he was born around midnight.

★ **1864:** Wilson's family was living in Georgia, where Wilson witnessed General Sherman's march through Georgia during the Civil War. The war had closed many schools, so Wilson didn't attend school until he was nine years old, but he was well taught at home.

★ **1873-1879:** At 17, Wilson entered Davidson College in North Carolina. He quit at the end of his first year to attend Princeton University (then called the College of New Jersey). At Princeton, he studied public speaking, became a leader in debating, and studied the lives of great American and British leaders. He graduated in 1879 and planned a career in public life. Upon graduation, Wilson dropped his given name: "Thomas."

★ **1879-1886:** He entered the University of Virginia Law School. In 1883 he entered Johns Hopkins University in Baltimore where he studied history and government. He published his first book in 1885 and received much praise from teachers and lawmakers about his writing on the federal government. He received a Ph.D. from Johns Hopkins in 1886.

On June 24, 1885, Wilson married Ellen Louise Axson. Between 1886 and 1889 the Wilsons had three daughters.

★ **1886-1890:** For three years Wilson was associate professor of history at Bryn Mawr College, near Philadelphia Pennsylvania. He and his family moved to Middletown, Connecticut, when he became professor of history and government at Wesleyan University. In 1890 he accepted a position at Princeton University to became a professor of law and politics.

Woodrow Wilson

TLC10394

★ **1902-1910:** Wilson became president of Princeton University. He struggled with faculty, students, and alumni to implement new ideas and modernize the university to make it a better place to learn. Articles about him were published in newspapers nation-wide. His name became well known, helping him enter politics.

★ **1910:** Wilson ran for governor of New Jersey and won. During his term he introduced reforms to get rid of dishonesty in the state government. The New Jersey legislature passed a primary election law, a law taxing public utility companies, and a law making employers responsible for their workers' injuries on the job.

★ **1912:** Wilson's planning and organization and his reputation as a successful reformer made him an ideal candidate to run for President for the Democratic Party. The Republican Party was divided: President Taft was running for a second term, and former President Roosevelt had also decided to run.

Wilson won with 435 electoral votes. His opponents' combined electoral votes were only 96.

★ **1913:** Wilson was inaugurated on March 4 at age 56.

Mrs. Wilson proposed cleaning up the slums in Washington, D.C., and Congress appropriated funds for the project.

★ **1914:** Mrs. Wilson became ill; she died on August 6.

As President, Wilson was successful in getting Congress to lower tariff rates. The Federal Trade Commission and Federal Reserve System, which set up a central banking system, were established. Congress also passed child labor laws and the Adamson Act which meant railroad workers could no longer be forced to work more than eight hours a day. Other workers soon received the same right.

Following the 16th Amendment to the Constitution, Congress enacted a federal income tax.

When World War I began in August 1914, Wilson focused on keeping the U.S. neutral while trying to maintain freedom of trade on the high seas.

Ellen Wilson

★ **)15:** On December 18, Wilson remarried. His new wife was Edith Bolling Galt of Washington, D.C.

A German submarine torpedoed and sank the British passenger ship *Lusitania* killing 128 Americans.

★ **1916:** Using the slogan, "He kept us out of war" Wilson campaigned for re-election. He won by 23 electoral votes. The U.S. didn't stay out of war much longer.

★ **1917:** Although Wilson refused to go to war in 1915 when Germany sank the *Lusitania*, he was forced to join World War I when Germany attacked U.S. merchant ships in the Atlantic Ocean.

The U.S. officially entered World War I when Congress declared war on April 6.

Wilson introduced the Selective Service. Men 21 to 30 years old had to register for the military. The age range was extended from 18 to 45 the following year. Those who were called to serve were determined by lottery.

★ **1918:** On January 8, Wilson gave his famous speech listing his Fourteen Points to be used as a guide for a peace settlement. The points included the formation of an association of nations to work together for world peace.

From October 6 to November 9, Wilson worked to negotiate an end to the war with Germany. On November 9, Kaiser Wilhelm II gave up control of the German government. Two days later peace was negotiated.

After peace was announced, he met with leaders from France, Great Britain and Italy. They agreed to accept his plan to establish the League of Nations, but he was forced to compromise on some of his Fourteen Points.

★ **1919:** From January 18 to June 28, Wilson helped draft the Treaty of Versailles at the Paris Peace Conference.

He returned to the U.S., hoping the Senate would accept the Treaty of Versailles and make the United States a member of the League of Nations. To his great disappointment, Congress rejected the treaty and America's membership in the League of Nations.

66

In September Wilson went on a 10-day speaking tour hoping to win support from Americans. He was overworked and his health was weak. On September 25, he collapsed from fatigue and nervous tension. On October 2, Wilson had a paralyzing stroke.

He was an invalid for the rest of his life but did not resign from office. His wife guided his hand when he signed official papers. His cabinet carried on official government business during his illness.

In November, Wilson watched from his bed as his Treaty was defeated.

The 18th Amendment banning the manufacture, transportation and sale of alcoholic beverages became law.

⭐ **1920:** The Treaty came up for a vote again in March. Once again it failed to win approval.

Wilson insisted the Treaty and the League be the chief issues of the 1920 presidential campaign. The Democrats favored it; the Republicans opposed it.

In the election, Republican Warren G. Harding defeated the Democratic candidate James M. Cox.

The League of Nations was established but the United States never joined. This was a major defeat for Wilson.

On December 10, he was awarded the 1919 Nobel Peace Prize for his work in establishing the League of Nations and seeking a fair peace agreement.

The 19th Amendment giving women the right to vote became law.

⭐ **1921-1924:** For almost three years after he left office, Wilson lived in Washington, D.C. He had some recovery but was unable to work. He accepted the defeat of his League of Nations with dignity but firmly believed in his plan for peace. His vision for a world peace organization was realized in 1945 when the United States took the lead in establishing the United Nations.

⭐ **1924:** Wilson died on February 3 at age 67. He was buried in Washington Cathedral and is the only President buried in Washington, D.C.

Warren Gamaliel Harding

29ᵗʰ President of the United States

Term: 1921-1923
Party: Republican

★★★★★★★★★★★★★★★★★★★★★★★★★★★★★★★★★★★★

★ **1865:** Warren G. Harding was born on November 2 near Corsica (now Blooming Grove), Ohio.

★ **1879:** At age 14, he studied at Ohio Central College. He joined the debate club and started the school's newspaper. In the next few years, Harding held a variety of jobs but didn't succeed at any. Journalism, public speaking, and politics interested him most.

★ **1884:** With two partners, he bought the *Marion Star*, a bankrupt daily newspaper.

★ **1891:** On July 8, he married Florence Kling DeWolfe, the daughter of a local banking family. She helped him turn the newspaper into a successful business and encouraged him to get involved in politics.

★ **1898:** Harding was elected to the Ohio legislature as a Republican.

★ **1903:** His next political post was lieutenant governor of Ohio.

★ **1910:** Harding ran for governor of Ohio but lost the election.

★ **1912:** He was chosen to nominate President Taft for a second term at the Republican National Convention.

★ **1914:** Harding was elected to the U.S. Senate. He served for six years but didn't introduce any major legislation. He favored high tariffs, opposed the League of Nations, and missed nearly half of the Senate roll calls for voting.

★ **1920:** Urged by his wife and Harry Daugherty, a politician and Republican supporter, Harding became a compromise candidate for President. Governor Calvin Coolidge of Massachusetts was his running mate.

In his campaign he avoided controversial issues and promised a return to "normalcy," the untroubled times before World War I. He liked making speeches and shaking hands.

Warren G. Harding

TLC10394

At a White House dinner

Harding won an overwhelming victory. It was the first presidential election that women voted in and the first one in which election returns were broadcast by radio.

⭐ **1921:** At 55, he became the first President to ride to his inauguration in an automobile.

Having little political experience, Harding depended on his cabinet to make most of the important decisions. This showed his poor judgment; it was soon discovered that several friends he had appointed were dishonest.

Harding signed peace treaties that did not include the United States joining the League of Nations.

The 18th Amendment banning the manufacture and sale of alcoholic beverages had been in effect for one year. However, at the White House Harding's dinner guests had alcoholic drinks.

Congress placed quotas on immigration for the first time.

⭐ **1922:** Congress raised tariffs to the highest levels ever.

Harding's lack of leadership became more evident.

⭐ **1923:** Secretary of the Interior Albert B. Fall accepted a bribe for leasing government owned oil fields to private companies. It became known as the Teapot Dome scandal and was the biggest scandal in Harding's administration.

Other scandals involving Harding's cabinet members became known and showed he had been a poor judge of character.

Although he was not directly involved in any of the scandals, Harding was concerned about his reputation. He went on a speaking tour to Alaska and the Pacific Northwest. On the trip, he received further news of scandals involving bribery and the stealing of government funds.

On the trip home, he became ill in Seattle. At age 57, he died in San Francisco on August 2.

News of the latest scandals had not yet been made public. Americans grieved the President's death, then were shocked to learn of more wrongdoings in his administration.

QUOTAS ON IMMIGRATION

John Calvin Coolidge

30th President of the United States

Term: 1923-1929
Party: Republican

★ **1872:** John Calvin Coolidge was born on July 4 in Plymouth Notch, Vermont. He dropped the name "John" after graduating college.

★ **1895:** He graduated from Amherst College cum laude and began to study with a law firm in Northampton, Massachusetts.

★ **1897:** Coolidge passed the bar exam and opened his own law office. Like many other Presidents who had been lawyers, he became involved in politics.

★ **1898:** He was elected to the Northampton city council and became city solicitor in 1900.

★ **1905:** On October 4, Coolidge married Grace Anna Goodhue, a teacher of the deaf.

★ **1906:** He was elected to the Massachusetts House of Representatives and was re-elected the following year.

★ **1909:** Coolidge was elected mayor of Northampton.

★ **1912-1915:** He served in the state senate.

★ **1915:** Voters elected him lieutenant governor of Massachusetts. He was re-elected twice.

★ **1918:** He was elected governor of Massachusetts.

★ **1919:** On the second day of a Boston police strike, Coolidge called in the state militia. In settling the strike, he made a statement that brought him national attention.

★ **1920:** The Republican Party chose him as the vice presidential candidate to run with Warren Harding. Upon winning the election, Harding invited Coolidge to attend cabinet meetings. He became the first Vice President to do so.

Calvin Coolidge

TLC10394

"Ladies and gentlemen... the President of the United States!"

1921: Coolidge became a life trustee of Amherst College.

1923: While visiting his father in Vermont, he received news of President Harding's death. He was the sixth Vice President to become President upon the death of a chief executive. Coolidge's father, a notary public and Justice of the Peace, swore his son in as President. More than two weeks later, Coolidge was sworn in a second time by a justice of the Supreme Court.

Coolidge became President as the Teapot Dome scandal in Harding's administration became public. He did not protect those who were guilty, and he made them resign. His greatest challenge as President was to clean up the scandals from Harding's time in office.

1924: After a year in office, Coolidge ran for president and won his own term. The economy was good and stock prices on Wall Street reached new highs. Farm prices, however, began to fall and farmers did not share in the nation's economic prosperity.

One of the Coolidges' two sons, age 16, died from an infection.

1925: For the first time, Americans listened to a President's inauguration speech on the radio.

Coolidge supported high tariffs to help American manufacturers. He reduced taxes and the national debt and encouraged the American people to invest in the stock market.

He was frugal and stressed economy to the White House staff.

1927: Coolidge announced he would not run for another term.

1929-1933: In 1929, he became a director of the New York Life Insurance Company. He continued his work as a trustee of Amherst College.

Coolidge and his wife retired to their home, called The Beeches, in Northampton, where Coolidge wrote his autobiography and a daily newspaper column.

He was greatly distressed by the stock market crash in October 1929 and the resulting economic depression.

On January 5, 1933, at age 60 Coolidge died in his home of a heart attack. He was buried in Vermont in Plymouth Notch cemetery where six generations of Coolidges are buried.

1957: Grace Coolidge died.

Herbert Clark Hoover

31st President of the United States

Term: 1929-1933
Party: Republican

⭐ **1874:** Herbert Clark Hoover was born on August 10 in West Branch, Iowa. He was the first President born west of the Mississippi.

⭐ **1880-1889:** Hoover's father died when he was six; his mother died when he was 10. Hoover was separated from his brother and sister and went to live with an aunt and uncle in Oregon. He quit high school at 15 and worked in a real estate office until he became interested in mining and engineering.

⭐ **1891-1895:** He worked his way through Stanford University in California to earn a degree in geology and mining engineering. He was in the school's first graduating class. While attending Stanford he met his future wife Lou Henry. She was the first woman to major in geology at Stanford.

⭐ **1897:** Hoover took a job managing gold mines in Australia.

⭐ **1898:** He accepted the position of chief engineer for the Chinese Imperial Bureau of Mines in China.

⭐ **1899:** Hoover married Lou Henry on February 10.

⭐ **1908:** He established his own mining business. With his wife and two young sons, he traveled to many parts of the world. Within six years he was a wealthy man.

⭐ **1914:** When World War I began, Hoover was in England. He helped 120,000 stranded Americans return home. He was made chairman of the American Relief Committee in Europe and helped get food to the Belgian and French people after German troops had taken over those two countries.

Herbert Hoover

TLC10394

I'm Hooverized!

⭐ **1917:** When the United States entered the war, President Wilson appointed Hoover director of the new U.S. Food Administration. Hoover organized the distribution of food and supplies throughout Europe during the war. Americans "Hooverized" to help send food to Europe.

⭐ **1921:** President Harding appointed Hoover Secretary of Commerce. He helped establish safety rules for automobiles and trains and worked to set safety standards for workers in factories.

Because of Hoover's outstanding work in public service, new President Coolidge kept Hoover as Secretary of Commerce.

⭐ **1928:** When Coolidge decided not to seek re-election, the Republican Party—and most Americans—turned to Hoover.

Hoover ran against Democrat Alfred E. Smith and won an overwhelming victory. He became President at a time of great prosperity in the United States.

⭐ **1929:** The Hoovers moved into the White House and lived in grand style paying for many fine services with their own money.

Although businesses continued to prosper, farmers faced hard times. Hoover created the Federal Farm Board to help them.

Seven months after Hoover bcame President, the stock market crashed on October 24. The date became known as Black Thursday. It was the beginning of the Great Depression.

⭐ **1930:** Many factories and banks closed; thousands of people were out of work. Farmers faced the loss of their farms. Hoover believed local and state government, not federal programs, should provide relief to the jobless. Congress later agreed to grant federal loans to states for relief measures.

During his administration, about 800 new public buildings were constructed to provide work. The Boulder Dam on the Colorado River was built and later renamed Hoover Dam.

Thank you, President Hoover!

1929: President Hoover creates Federal Farm Board!

⭐ **1932:** As Hoover neared the end of his term, the economy did not improve. He cut taxes to help solve the depression, but banks continued to fail and unemployment continued to increase. Americans blamed the President for their poverty, and he became unpopular.

When 15,000 veterans marched in Washington to cash in their war bonus certificates because of tough economic times, Hoover had the veterans removed by troops. He became more unpopular.

He lost the presidential re-election to Democrat Franklin Delano Roosevelt and retired from public life.

⭐ **1933:** In February, the 20th Amendment known as the "lame duck amendment" became law. It went into effect in October of that year. It changed the last day of a President's term to January 20 instead of March 4. Hoover was the last "lame duck" President.

After leaving office Hoover retired from public life. He and Mrs. Hoover moved from California to New York City.

⭐ **1946:** Hoover came out of retirement. After World War II ended, President Truman named him chairman of the Famine Emergency Commission.

⭐ **1947:** He headed the Hoover Commission to help reorganize government agencies and cut costs.

⭐ **1951-1964:** Hoover published his memoirs. He also wrote *The Ordeal of Woodrow Wilson* and several other books. He became a trustee or director of nine private educational, charitable, and scientific institutions.

He gave all his income from government employment to public service agencies and projects.

Hoover died on October 20 at age 90 and was buried near his birthplace in West Branch, Iowa.

Franklin Delano Roosevelt

32nd President of the United States

Term: 1933-1945
Party: Democratic

★★

★ **1882:** Franklin Delano Roosevelt was born on January 30 in Hyde Park, New York. He became the first and last person to be elected to four terms as President.

★ **1896:** When he was 14, he entered Groton, a private school in Massachusetts. Until this time he had been taught by tutors at home.

★ **1900-1904:** Roosevelt attended Harvard University and studied history. In 1903 he was appointed editor of the school newspaper, the *Harvard Crimson.* During his time at Harvard, his cousin Theodore Roosevelt was President of the United States.

★ **1904-1907:** He attended Columbia Law School and became a lawyer in 1907.

★ **1905:** Roosevelt married Anna Eleanor Roosevelt, a distant cousin on March 17. President Theodore Roosevelt came up from Washington to give the bride away.

★ **1910:** Influenced by his cousin Theodore, Franklin Roosevelt also decided on a career in politics. He became active in the Democratic Party and was elected to the New York state senate.

★ **1912:** Roosevelt supported Woodrow Wilson against his cousin Theodore Roosevelt in the presidential election.

★ **1913:** Wilson won and appointed Roosevelt Assistant Secretary of the Navy. Roosevelt held this position throughout World War I.

★ **1918:** He toured battlefields and met with military leaders in Europe.

★ **1920:** Roosevelt became a vice presidential candidate with James Cox. They lost to Republicans Warren Harding and Calvin Coolidge.

Franklin D. Roosevelt

1921: While vacationing with his family at their home on Campobello Island, Roosevelt was stricken with polio and his legs were paralyzed. Although he recovered, he had to use braces, canes, or a wheelchair for the rest of his life. Many thought his career in politics was over, but Roosevelt continued on.

1928: He was elected governor of New York and was re-elected two years later.

1929-1932: These were the years of the Great Depression. Banks failed, businesses closed, and thousands of Americans lost their jobs. President Hoover hoped conditions would improve on their own. He disappointed the American people by not doing enough to help them. Americans were looking for a new, strong leader.

Roosevelt ran for President promising a "New Deal" to Americans. His vice presidential running mate was Speaker of the House of Representatives John Nance Garner.

Roosevelt became the first President to make an acceptance speech at a national political convention.

People had confidence and sang "Happy Days Are Here Again."

1933: On February 15 before Roosevelt took the oath of office, Guiseppe Zangara tried to assassinate him. Roosevelt escaped injury, but the mayor of Chicago was killed by a gunshot.

Roosevelt defeated Hoover in a landslide victory and promptly began his plan to try to improve economic conditions.

Congress began a special session called the "Hundred Days" to pass recovery and reform laws. It gave Americans hope and confidence. Federal work programs created thousands of jobs.

Government projects made the national debt higher than ever. Taxes were increased and bonds were sold to raise money. Roosevelt spoke to the American people regularly by radio. He called these talks "fireside chats."

He appointed Frances Perkins as Secretary of Labor. She was the first woman appointed to a cabinet post.

Eleanor Roosevelt became the first First Lady to become active and work for humanitarian causes.

Eleanor Roosevelt

★ **1935:** The Social Security Act was passed by Congress.

★ **1936:** Roosevelt was re-elected for a second term. John Nance Garner was again his Vice President.

★ **1939:** World War II began when Germany invaded Poland.

★ **1940:** The American people broke tradition and Roosevelt was elected to a third term as President. Secretary of Agriculture Henry A. Wallace was his Vice President.

The French Army surrendered to Germany shocking America.

★ **1941:** Japan attacked Pearl Harbor on December 7. On December 8, President Roosevelt declared war, and the United States entered World War II.

★ **1944:** Historians say Roosevelt wanted to retire, but he felt it was his duty not to do so during wartime. He won his fourth term and Senator Harry S. Truman of Missouri became the new Vice President.

Congress approved the "GI Bill of Rights."

★ **1945:** Two days after being inaugurated for the fourth time, Roosevelt attended the Yalta Conference with Prime Minister of Great Britain Winston Churchill and Russian leader Joseph Stalin.

The war was nearing an end, but on April 12, tired and in weakened health, Roosevelt died suddenly at his retreat in Warm Springs, Georgia. He was 63 years old. He was buried at his home in Hyde Park, New York.

Eleanor Roosevelt continued her role in public life and served as a delegate to the United Nations. In 1948 she helped write the Universal Declaration of Human Rights. She died in 1962 and was buried alongside her husband at Hyde Park.

That's good news!

1935: Social Security Act passed.

Harry S. Truman

33rd President of the United States

Term: 1945-1953
Party: Democratic

★★★

★ **1884:** Harry S. Truman was born on May 8 in Lamar, Missouri.

★ **1898:** As a boy, Truman wore glasses and stayed out of rough play and sports. He spent time in the library and by 14 had read all the books in the Independence Public Library.

★ **1901-1905:** He graduated from high school, but his parents could not afford to send him to college. In Independence, Truman worked as a bank clerk, theater usher, and piano player.

★ **1906-1917:** His father, unable to manage his farm by himself any longer, asked Truman to come home to help. For the next 11 years Truman helped manage the farm. In the evenings, he often went to Democratic Party meetings. He served on the local school board and joined the National Guard.

★ **1917:** When World War I began, Truman enlisted in the army. He fought in some of the most dangerous battles in France as a field artillery officer and rose to the rank of colonel.

★ **1919:** When he returned from Europe, Truman married his childhood sweetheart, Elizabeth "Bess" Wallace. They were married on June 28. That year, Truman and a friend opened a men's clothing store. They ran it for two years, but the business failed in the 1921 recession.

★ **1922:** Truman was elected judge of Jackson County, Missouri. He served several terms and became known for his honesty.

★ **1934:** He was elected to the U.S. Senate.

Harry S. Truman

On May 7, the Germans surrendered, ending World War II in Europe.

The war with Germany was ended, but the war with Japan continued. One of Truman's first major decisions was to drop atomic bombs on Hiroshima and Nagasaki, Japan. On August 6, an atomic bomb was dropped on Hiroshima. On August 9, a second bomb hit Nagasaki. Japan surrendered shortly after, on September 2.

The United Nations was established on October 24. For the first time, the U.S. was part of a world organization.

⭐ **1946:** The Cold War between the U.S. and Russia began.

Republicans won control of Congress and blocked most of Truman's measures.

May 7, 1945 – Germany surrenders. WWII in Europe is over.

⭐ **1941:** Truman was appointed chairman of the Committee to Investigate the National Defense Program. He established a national reputation when the committee's recommendations saved the nation billions of dollars in the defense industry.

⭐ **1944:** When President Franklin Roosevelt ran for a fourth term, he selected Truman as his vice presidential running mate.

⭐ **1945:** On April 12, just 83 days after becoming Vice President, Truman became President after President Roosevelt's sudden death.

Plans to establish the United Nations had just begun. The first U.N. conference met in San Francisco 13 days after Truman was sworn in.

The Cold War between the U.S. & Russia began in 1946.

★ **1947:** Truman announced the Truman Doctrine, guaranteeing aid to nations resisting Communism.

★ **1948:** The Marshall Plan extended the Truman Doctrine and began giving economic aid to war-torn countries in Europe.

Truman ran for a second term and won the election.

Reconstruction of the White House began when it was discovered its structure was weak. The Truman Balcony was built behind the pillars of the south portico. The First Family moved to Blair House and lived there until 1952.

★ **1949:** In the spring, the U.S. and 11 other nations signed the North Atlantic Treaty Organization (NATO). Other countries joined later to defend western Europe.

★ **1950:** When Communist forces from North Korea invaded South Korea on June 25, Truman sent armed forces to aid South Korea.

On November 1 two Puerto Rican nationalists attempted to assassinate Truman in Blair House. One Secret Service guard was killed and one was injured.

Truman established a program called the Fair Deal to reform U.S. domestic problems.

There were charges of communist spies in the federal government.

★ **1952:** Truman announced he would not seek re-election.

★ **1953:** Truman retired to his home in Independence, Missouri, and wrote his memoirs. He continued to be active in the Democratic Party.

★ **1957:** The Harry S. Truman Library opened in Independence.

★ **1972:** After a short illness in December, Truman died on December 26 at age 88. He was buried in the Truman Library courtyard.

TLC10394

Dwight David Eisenhower

34th President of the United States

Term: 1953-1961
Party: Republican

★★★★★★★★★★★★★★★★★★★★★★★★★★★★★★★★★★★★★★★

★ **1890:** Dwight David Eisenhower was born on October 14 in Denison, Texas. His family moved to Abilene, Kansas, before he was 2. He acquired the nickname "Ike" when he was a child.

★ **1911-1915:** Eisenhower became a cadet at the U.S. Military Academy at West Point. In 1915, he graduated as a second lieutenant and was posted to Fort Sam Houston near San Antonio, Texas. He met Mamie Geneva Doud that year.

★ **1916:** Eisenhower and Mamie were married on July 1, the same day he was promoted to first lieutenant.

During World War I, Eisenhower directed tank training programs for officers and recruits at Camp Colt in Gettysburg, Pennsylvania.

★ **1926:** After serving at several army posts, Eisenhower graduated from the Command and General Staff School at Fort Leavenworth, Kansas. He graduated first in his class of 275.

★ **1933:** He became an aide to General Douglas MacArthur, the U.S. Army chief of staff.

★ **1935:** As the Philippines prepared for independence, Eisenhower planned the commonwealth's military defense.

★ **1941:** After attending the Army War College in Washington, D.C., Eisenhower was promoted to colonel in March and then brigadier general in September.

★ **1942:** In March, he was promoted to major general; in July, he was promoted to lieutenant general.

Six months after the United States entered World War II, Army Chief of Staff General George C. Marshall appointed Eisenhower as Commander General of the U.S. forces. He beat 366 senior army officers for the post.

You can call me Ike!

as a boy the nickname "Ike" sticks.

Dwight D. Eisenhower

⭐ **1943:** In February, Eisenhower was promoted to the rank of four-star general. He was later named Supreme Commander of the Allied Expeditionary Force in Europe. He organized the Allied invasions of Sicily and of Italy and won praise for creating unity among commanders of different nations.

⭐ **1944:** On June 4, he commanded Operation Overlord, the largest seaborne invasion in history. With fairness, tact and respect, he led the troops and leaders of the U.S., Great Britain, and other allies as a unified fighting force. Known as the D-Day invasion, the victory at Normandy led to Germany's surrender 11 months later.

On December 10, Eisenhower was promoted to the newly created rank of five-star general.

⭐ **1945:** Germany surrendered on May 7.

Eisenhower was made Chief of Staff of the U.S. Army and oversaw reorganizing the army for peace.

⭐ **1948-1950:** He left the army to become president of Columbia University. During this time he wrote a book, *Crusade in Europe*, about his wartime experiences; it became a best-seller.

He wasn't out of uniform for long. Eisenhower returned to the army and was named Supreme Commander of North Atlantic Treaty Organization (NATO) forces in Europe.

⭐ **1952:** Although he had been approached by both the Democratic and Republican Parties to run for President in 1948, Eisenhower had refused. In 1952, he declared himself a Republican and became a presidential candidate. His running mate was Richard Nixon.

Eisenhower's experience and integrity, his friendly grin and folksy manner, and his ability to lead armies won voters over easily. In November, he was elected President.

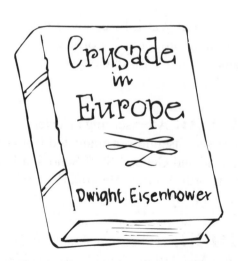

Crusade in Europe

Dwight Eisenhower

TLC10394

★ **1953:** His first success as President was to help end the Korean War. A truce was signed on July 27.

As President, Eisenhower led as he did in the army and delegated wide powers to his aides.

He created the Department of Health, Education and Welfare.

His Atoms for Peace program promoted peaceful uses of nuclear energy.

★ **1954:** The Supreme Court ruled racial segregation in public schools was unconstitutional.

★ **1955:** In September, Eisenhower had a heart attack but recovered fairly quickly.

★ **1956:** He handled the Suez Canal crisis with Britain, France, and Israel effectively. He gave voters confidence to re-elect him.

★ **1957:** He sent federal troops to Little Rock, Arkansas, to enforce the integration of the city's high school.

Eisenhower was disappointed when Russia launched the satellite *Sputnik I* on October 4, beating the U.S. in the space race.

★ **1958:** On January 31, America launched its first satellite, *Explorer I*. Six months later, Congress established the National Aeronautics and Space Administration (NASA) for further space exploration.

★ **1959:** Fidel Castro established a Communist government in Cuba.

Alaska and Hawaii became the 49th and 50th states.

Soviet Premier Nikita Khrushchev came to the U.S. in September. It was the first visit to the U.S. by a top Soviet leader.

★ **1960:** Castro seized all property owned by American companies in Cuba.

In May, Russians shot down an American U-2 reconnaissance plane over Soviet territory. Eisenhower admitted such planes had been in use for four years.

★ **1961:** Eisenhower ended diplomatic relations with Cuba on January 3.

He was the first President whose term of office was limited by the 22nd Amendment which became law in 1951.

When his term ended, the Eisenhowers retired to a farm they bought in Gettysburg, Pennsylvania.

★ **1969:** On March 28, at age 78, Eisenhower died of heart failure in a Washington, D.C., hospital. He was buried in Abilene, Kansas. Ten years later Mamie was laid to rest beside him.

1954: The Supreme Court ruled racial segregation in public schools was unconstitutional.

John Fitzgerald Kennedy

35th President of the United States

Term: 1961-1963
Party: Democratic

★ **1917:** John Fitzgerald Kennedy was born on May 29 in Brookline, Massachusetts. At 43, he was the youngest person ever elected President, and at 46 he was the youngest to die in office. He was the first U.S. President born in the 20th century.

Kennedy grew up in a large family of nine children. His mother was the daughter of the mayor of Boston; his father had served as U.S. ambassador to Great Britain.

★ **1936:** After graduating from Choate Academy in Connecticut, he entered Harvard University.

★ **1939:** In the shadow of World War II, during the spring and summer, Kennedy toured Europe. From his travels he wrote *Why England Slept*, a book detailing why England was unprepared for the war.

★ **1940:** Kennedy graduated from Harvard University cum laude.

★ **1941-1943:** He served as a naval officer in the South Pacific in World War II and was assigned to a PT boat squadron late in 1942. In August 1943, he escaped death when a Japanese destroyer cut PT-109, the boat he commanded, in half. He received the Navy and Marine Corps Medal

for heroism and leadership in keeping his crew together until they were rescued. He received the Purple Heart for being wounded in combat.

★ **1944:** Kennedy's older brother Joe was killed in a flying mission.

★ **1946:** Kennedy's political career began when he was elected to the U.S. House of Representatives from Massachusetts. He served for three terms.

★ **1951:** He met his future wife Jacqueline Bouvier.

John F. Kennedy

1961: President Kennedy establishes the U.S. Peace Corps.

★ **1952:** He was elected a U.S. senator.

★ **1953:** Kennedy married Jacqueline Bouvier on September 12 in Newport, Rhode Island.

★ **1954-1955:** While recovering from two back surgeries, Kennedy wrote *Profiles in Courage*. The book won the Pulitzer Prize for biography in 1957.

★ **1956:** Kennedy tried but failed to win the Democratic vice presidential nomination. He began to set his sights on a presidential nomination for the 1960 election.

★ **1958:** He was re-elected to the U.S. Senate.

★ **1960:** After winning many primary victories, Kennedy won the Democratic nomination at the national convention in Los Angeles. Lyndon B. Johnson of Texas, who had also tried for the nomination, became Kennedy's vice presidential running mate.

Kennedy's opponent was former Vice President Richard Nixon. Nixon was better known, but Kennedy was knowledgeable and confident.

Kennedy won a close election.

★ **1961:** At 44 years of age, Kennedy was inaugurated on January 20. With a three-year-old daughter and an infant son, Kennedy and his wife brought youth, energy, and vigor to the White House.

The programs Kennedy proposed were known as the New Frontier.

Demands for equal rights for African Americans was one of the major domestic issues of his administration.

One of Kennedy's most successful programs, the U.S. Peace Corps, was established.

★ **1962:** In October, Russian Soviet missiles were discovered in Cuba. Kennedy ordered the Russians to dismantle the missiles. He ordered the U.S. Navy to blockade Cuba. The threat of nuclear war was real and the Cuban missile crisis threatened world peace. Finally, Soviet Premier Khrushchev ordered the missiles removed.

★ **1963:** Kennedy signed a treaty with Russia and Great Britain banning the testing of nuclear weapons in the atmosphere, outer space, and under water.

When Communist North Vietnam threatened to invade South Vietnam and Thailand, Kennedy sent military advisers.

To demonstrate the demand for equal rights for African Americans, a Freedom March of 200,000 individuals was held in Washington, D.C. Kennedy asked Congress to pass legislation requiring restaurants and hotels to admit people regardless of race.

On November 22, when Kennedy was on a political trip to Dallas, Texas, an assassin named Lee Harvey Oswald fired shots at President Kennedy's motorcade, killing him. The nation and the world were shocked.

Two days later, Oswald was shot while being transported from a city jail to a county jail. The shooting was seen on national television.

Vice President Lyndon Johnson took the oath of office aboard the plane carrying Kennedy's body back to Washington, D.C. The flag-draped coffin was carried to the Capitol Rotunda to lie in state as thousands of mourners filed past.

Representatives from over 90 countries attended the funeral on November 25. Americans watched the procession on television. Mrs. Kennedy was admired by people the world over for her courage and dignity through the tragedy.

President Kennedy was buried with full military honors at Arlington National Cemetery.

★ **1964:** Chief Justice Earl Warren headed an investigation of the assassination. A committee reported Oswald had acted alone. Others disputed this finding and believed Oswald was part of a group that planned to kill Kennedy.

During the 1970s, a special U.S. House of Representatives committee re-examined the assassination evidence. They accepted evidence of sound experts who claimed shots were fired at the motorcade from two locations at the same time. In 1978, the committee concluded that Kennedy was probably assassinated as the result of a conspiracy.

In 1982, the National Research Council disagreed with the House committee's finding.

★ **1994:** On May 19, Jacqueline Kennedy Onassis died of cancer. She was buried alongside President Kennedy at Arlington National Cemetery.

★ **1999:** On July 16, Kennedy's 38-year-old son John F. Kennedy, Jr., his wife Carolyn, and her sister were killed when a plane Kennedy was flying crashed in the Atlantic Ocean near Martha's Vineyard.

1963 ~ The Freedom March

Lyndon Baines Johnson

36th President of the United States

Term: 1963-1969
Party: Democratic

★ **1908:** Lyndon Baines Johnson was born August 27 near Stonewall, Texas.

★ **1918:** Even as a child, Johnson liked to talk. He got his first job shining shoes at age 10 at a local barbershop. Here he overheard men talking politics, which interested him. He enjoyed accompanying his father to the capital of Austin, where the elder Johnson served in the Texas legislature for 10 years. Johnson found he enjoyed government and politics.

★ **1923:** He graduated high school at 15 and went to California, where he worked as a laborer picking oranges and washing cars. He returned to Texas and worked with a road-building crew. He decided he didn't want to do manual labor for his life's work.

★ **1927:** Johnson entered Southwest Texas State College and worked his way through as a janitor and as secretary to the college president. He enjoyed campus politics and became a star debater.

★ **1930-1932:** Johnson took time off and taught Mexican American students in the town of Cotulla for one year to earn enough money to finish college. He graduated and then spent a year teaching debate and public speaking at Sam Houston High School in Houston.

Texas congressman Richard M. Kleberg took 23-year-old Johnson to Washington, D.C., where Johnson worked as his secretary. Johnson began to earn a solid political education.

★ **1934:** Johnson met Claudia Alta Taylor , who went by the name "Lady Bird." They were married on November 17. Eventually they had two daughters. All four Johnsons had the same initials, LBJ.

★ **1935:** President Roosevelt made Johnson head of the New Deal National Youth Administration in Texas. His job was to help young unemployed people find jobs during the depression.

Lyndon B. Johnson

1953-1960: JOHNSON LED THE FIGHT TO CREATE SOCIAL WELFARE PROGRAMS TO HELP THE POOR...

THAT'S GOOD! I'M GETTING TIRED OF LIVING OUT OF GARBAGE CANS!

⭐ **1937:** Johnson was elected to the House of Representatives and developed a lasting friendship with President Roosevelt.

⭐ **1941-1942:** Three days after the U.S. declared war on Japan, Johnson was sworn in as a lieutenant commander. He was the first congressman to go into uniform. He served in the Pacific fleet until President Roosevelt called all members of Congress home in July 1942.

⭐ **1948:** He was elected to the Senate and served three terms.

⭐ **1953-1960:** Johnson became the Democratic minority leader in the Senate in 1953 and the majority leader in 1955. During this time, he led the fight for the Civil Rights Act and supported social welfare programs to help the poor.

He sponsored the law that established the National Aeronautical and Space Administration (NASA).

In 1957 he put through the first civil rights measure in 80 years. In 1960, another civil rights measure was passed.

He became a presidential candidate in 1960. When Kennedy won the election, Johnson became Vice President and resigned from the Senate.

⭐ **1961-1963:** He took a more active role than any previous Vice President. He served as chairperson of the NASA council, the Peace Corps National Advisory Council, the President's Committee on Equal Opportunity Employment, and the National Security Council.

When President Kennedy was assassinated on November 22, Johnson became President of a saddened and shocked nation. As *Air Force One* sat on the tarmac in Dallas, ready to take Kennedy's body back to Washington, Johnson took the oath of office. Beside him were his wife and President Kennedy's widow.

He became the fourth Vice President to succeed to the presidency because of an assassination. He also became the first southern President in the 20th century.

Lady Bird Johnson made the beautification of interstate highways and of the national capital her main projects as First Lady.

1961-1963: LADYBIRD JOHNSON HELPS BEAUTIFY OUR HIGHWAYS.

1964-1969: PRESIDENT JOHNSON RAISES THE MINIMUM WAGE...

YES!

⭐ **1964:** Johnson ran for re-election and won in a landslide.

⭐ **1964-1968:** The U.S. became more involved in the war in Vietnam after North Vietnam torpedo boats attacked U.S. Navy destroyers in the Gulf of Tonkin. In 1966, 400,000 soldiers were in Vietnam and bombing had increased.

Johnson introduced his Great Society program. He worked to pass new laws to help eliminate poverty, improve the educational system, and aid older citizens. He introduced Medicare and the Voting Rights Act. He raised the minimum hourly wage, and introduced laws to protect consumers and the environment. A law forbidding racial discrimination in hotels, restaurants, and other public places was passed.

Although civil rights laws had been passed, there was racial unrest. Riots broke out in several U.S. cities.

Johnson appointed Robert C. Weaver as the first African American cabinet member. Thurgood Marshall became the first African American to serve on the U.S. Supreme Court.

Three U.S. astronauts successfully orbited the moon in 1968.

By 1968, Johnson had become very unpopular because of the war in Vietnam. Republicans opposed his costly domestic programs as well as the war. He surprised the nation when he announced he would not seek another term as President.

He did, however, call for a reduction of bombing in North Vietnam. This led to peace talks in November.

⭐ **1970:** Johnson and Lady Bird retired to their ranch in Texas where he wrote his memoirs.

⭐ **1972:** Johnson had a heart attack in April and slowly recovered.

⭐ **1973:** On January 22, at age 64, Johnson had a fatal heart attack. He was buried in the cemetery on his ranch which is part of a national historic park.

After his death, the Manned Spacecraft Center at Houston was renamed the Lyndon B. Johnson Space Center.

1964-1968: THURGOOD MARSHALL BECOMES THE FIRST BLACK SUPREME COURT JUSTICE.

Richard Milhous Nixon

37th President of the United States

Term: 1969-1974
Party: Republican

⭐ **1913:** Richard Milhous Nixon was born on January 9 in Yorba Linda, California.

⭐ **1930-1934:** After becoming an excellent debater in high school, Nixon entered Whittier College where he was an outstanding history student. He was a good public speaker and spoke at many civic and community events. He had been offered scholarships to Harvard and Yale, but his parents could not afford the travel and living expenses so he attended a local college.

⭐ **1934-1937:** He attended Duke University Law School on a scholarship. After graduating from the North Carolina school he joined a law firm in California and later became a partner.

⭐ **1939:** At age 26, he became the youngest member of the Whittier College Board of Trustees.

⭐ **1940:** Nixon married Thelma Catherine (Pat) Ryan on June 21. They had met during tryouts for a community theater play in Whittier. Eventually they had two daughters, Tricia and Julie. Both daughters were married in the White House.

⭐ **1942-1945:** He went to work for the Office of Price Administration in Washington, D.C.. He then served on active duty with the Navy in the Pacific during World War II.

⭐ **1946:** As a Republican, Nixon won his first political office when he was elected to the U.S. House of Representatives from Cali-fornia. He was re-elected two years later. As a member of the House Committee on Un-American activities, he gained national attention for his prosecution of an alleged Communist spy, Alger Hiss, a former Department of State employee.

Richard M. Nixon

★ **1953-1961:** Nixon was a better Vice President than people thought he would be. He supported civil rights and worked to increase America's influence around the world. He toured nearly 60 countries and visited every continent except Antarctica. In Russia, he did well in a debate with Soviet Premier Nikita Khrushchev.

★ **1960:** When Eisenhower's second term ended, Nixon fought John Kennedy in the presidential election and lost by a narrow margin. Nixon moved back to California and set his sights on running for governor.

★ **1962:** He ran for governor of California and lost. He gave this famous statement to the press: "You won't have Dick Nixon to kick around anymore." Many politicians and Americans thought his political career was over.

★ **1963-1967:** He moved to New York City where he practiced law and was active in the Republican Party. He spoke at meetings and civic groups to keep his name public. He gained political support, improved his reputation, and won several presidential primaries, vowing to bring about peace in Vietnam.

★ **1950:** Nixon ran for and was elected to the U.S. Senate. His opponent was Helen Gahagan Douglas. Without having any proof, Nixon led people to believe she favored communism. He also told voters women should be at home, not in the Senate. Although Nixon won the campaign, it was labeled dirty and dishonest, and he was nicknamed "Tricky Dick."

★ **1952:** Although Nixon had a tarnished reputation, Dwight Eisenhower saw his good traits and chose Nixon as his vice presidential running mate. Nixon was almost let go after he was charged with using campaign funds for personal use during his Senate race. He went on national television to appeal to the public and was able to clear his name. This became known as the "Checkers" speech.

Eisenhower won the election and Nixon became Vice President.

WHERE ARE WE GOING?
BEATS ME.

1953-1961: NIXON VISITS EVERY CONTINENT EXCEPT ANTARCTICA.

DID SOMEBODY SAY "DRAFT"?

★ **1968:** Nixon won the Republican nomination for President. His vice presidential running mate was Governor Spiro Agnew of Maryland. Nixon won the election with a solid victory over Hubert H. Humphrey.

★ **1969:** He was inaugurated at age 56 and became the 12ᵗʰ former Vice President to become President. Nixon's immediate and major goal was settlement of the Vietnam War. There were protests about immediate vs. gradual withdrawal of forces.

On July 20 astronauts Neil Armstrong and Ed Aldrin became the first people to walk on the moon when *Apollo XI* landed there.

Congress passed Nixon's proposal for a lottery system for the military draft.

★ **1971:** Congress lowered the minimum voting age in all elections to 18.

★ **1972:** Nixon was easily elected to a second term.

He ordered a blockade of North Vietnam to cut off its war supplies from Russia and China. The U.S. began to withdraw troops from Vietnam.

Nixon visited the Soviet Union. During the visit he signed agreements with the leader of the Soviet Communist Party to limit the production of nuclear weapons.

Nixon's presidency began to fall apart soon after the election. It was discovered he had approved a break in at the Democratic National Committee headquarters at the Watergate Hotel. Illegal listening equipment had been planted to get campaign information. The "dirty tricks" campaign and Watergate scandal were the beginning of a long list of political wrongdoings in the Nixon administration.

Nixon worked to establish diplomatic relations with Communist China. He made a historic visit to China and became the first U.S. President to visit the country.

★ **1973:** On January 27, a cease-fire agreement was signed in Paris by the U.S., North Vietnam, South Vietnam, and the Viet Cong, ending U.S. involvement. On March 29, after the exchange of war prisoners was completed, the last U.S. forces left South Vietnam. (Both North and South Vietnam and the Viet Cong soon violated the cease-fire agreement and continued fighting. The end of the war came on April 30, 1975, when South Vietnam surrendered to Communist North Vietnam.)

Vice President Agnew was charged with accepting bribes and nonpayment of his income taxes while he held office in Maryland. Agnew resigned on October 10.

On December 6, Nixon appointed Gerald Ford to the vice presidency.

The continuing Watergate investigation became a main issue. Evidence was discovered connecting White House officials with the Watergate burglary and the hiding of information. Nixon denied any part in the break-in or the cover-up.

Nixon refused to turn over tape recordings he had made of conversations with his staff. Nixon fired Archibald Cox, the man heading the Watergate investigation. This led to a move for Nixon's impeachment. Hearings began in October.

⭐ **1974:** Edited taped conversations with his staff were released in April that weakened Nixon's case. In July, the House Judiciary Committee recommended impeachment on three counts.

In August, a taped conversation that took place on June 23, 1972, six days after the Watergate break-in, revealed Nixon was aware of the burglary and was involved in its cover-up.

Rather than face certain impeachment, Nixon resigned as President on August 9. He became the first U.S. President to resign from office. Gerald Ford took the oath of office on the same day.

About 40 persons were tried for crimes related to the Watergate break-in. Most resigned in disgrace and were convicted. President Ford pardoned Nixon on September 8, and Nixon escaped any legal consequences.

Nixon and his wife returned to their home in San Clemente, California, where he began to write his autobiography. In 1980, they moved to New York City; in 1981, they moved to New Jersey to be closer to their daughters and grandchildren. In addition to his biography, he wrote three other books about foreign policy, leaders, and Vietnam.

⭐ **1993:** Nixon's wife Pat died on June 22.

⭐ **1994:** Ten months later, on April 22, Nixon died of a stroke in New York City. He and Pat were buried in Yorba Linda, California, on the grounds of the Richard M. Nixon Library and Birthplace.

Gerald Rudolph Ford

38th President of the United States

Term: 1974-1977
Party: Republican

★★

★ **1913:** Gerald Rudolph Ford, Jr., was born as Leslie Lynch King, Jr., on July 14 in Omaha, Nebraska. He was renamed Gerald Rudolph Ford when he was four years old. His mother had divorced his father, returned to her hometown of Grand Rapids, Michigan, and remarried. When her new husband adopted her young son, she gave him the same name as her new husband.

★ **1931:** Ford became a star football player in high school. In his senior year he was voted most popular senior in all the city's high schools. His prize was a five-day trip to Washington, D.C. He got to visit Congress and the White House.

He also won a football scholarship to the University of Michigan and became the school's most valuable freshman football player.

★ **1935-1938:** After graduating, he was offered contracts by both the Green Bay Packers and the Detroit Lions to be a professional football player. He had decided to study law, but accepted a job as football coach at Yale University in order to save money for law school. In the summers, he worked as a park ranger at Yellowstone National Park to earn more money. He saved enough and entered Yale Law School.

★ **1941-1946:** After earning his law degree, he and a friend opened a law office in Grand Rapids. Shortly after, Japan bombed Pearl Harbor. Ford joined the Navy as an ensign and served in heavy combat in the Pacific. When he left the Navy almost four years later, he had won several medals and was a lieutenant commander.

Gerald R. Ford

★ **1946:** Ford rejoined the law firm in Grand Rapids and became active in Republican politics.

★ **1947:** Encouraged by his stepfather and a former senator who had helped establish the United Nations, Ford challenged a representative and ran for Congress. He was elected to the U.S. House of Representatives and was re- elected to 13 more terms.

While campaigning, Ford met Elizabeth "Betty" Bloomer.

★ **1948:** Ford and Betty were married on October 15. They moved to Washington, D.C., and Ford became close friends with Richard Nixon.

★ **1963:** While serving as a representative, President Lyndon Johnson appointed Ford to the seven-member Warren Commission investigating the assassination of President John F. Kennedy.

★ **1965:** He became House minority leader and earned a reputation as being a "team player."

★ **1967:** Ford supported President Johnson's early Vietnam War policies. With no sign of the war ending, Ford began to strongly attack the U.S.'s war strategy.

★ **1973:** Nixon's Vice President Spiro Agnew was accused of taking bribes and not paying his income taxes while he held office in Maryland. Agnew resigned. Acting under the 25th Amendment to the Constitution, Nixon appointed minority leader in the House of Representatives Gerald Ford to the vice presidency.

When Ford became Vice President, Nixon was facing deeper charges regarding the Watergate break-in scandal. Ford went on a national speaking tour and expressed his faith in Nixon.

First Lady Betty Ford

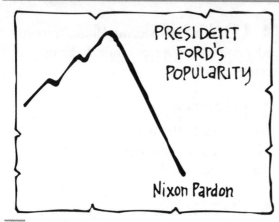

PRESIDENT FORD'S POPULARITY

Nixon Pardon

★ 1974: When Nixon resigned rather than face impeachment, Ford became President. He was the only person to serve as Vice President and President without being elected to either office. He had been Vice President for only eight months when he became President.

One month after Ford became President, his wife underwent surgery for breast cancer. Betty Ford was praised for publicly speaking about it.

Ford became President at a time when the U.S. had lost faith in the presidency and in politicians. The Vietnam War was still an issue, and there was an economic depression and high unemployment. But Ford had a warm, friendly manner and a reputation for honesty. The American people welcomed him.

Ford's popularity dropped a month after he became President when he granted Nixon a pardon for whatever crimes Nixon might have committed. This caused a major controversy as many Americans thought Nixon should be brought to trial and punished for crimes he committed as President.

Eight days after pardoning Nixon, Ford announced the Amnesty Program. Vietnam War draft dodgers and deserters could work in a public service job for up to two years. Only 22,000 out of 106,000 eligible people applied.

Ford did have successes. In the final days of the Vietnam War, when South Vietnam was taken over by Communist North Vietnam, Ford arranged for the evacuation of remaining U.S. citizens and many Vietnamese refugees. About 100,000 refugees came to the U.S. He took military action against Cambodia after Communist troops seized the U.S. merchant ship, *Mayaguez.*

★ 1975: Two attempted assassinations against Ford failed in September. Both assassins were women and were sentenced to life in prison.

★ 1976: Although former governor of California Ronald Reagan challenged Ford in some primaries and made a good showing, Ford won the nomination for Republican presidential candidate. His Democratic opponent was former governor of Georgia, Jimmy Carter. The election was close, but Ford lost to Carter.

★ 1977: On January 20, Ford left office and retired with his wife to Palm Springs, California. He remained active in Republican politics, served on the board of directors of several companies, and lectured at colleges and universities.

★ 2006: On December 26, Ford died of cerebrovascular disease at his home in Rancho Mirage, California. He was 93. He was the 11th president to lie in state in the Capitol Rotunda and was one of only four former presidents to live to 90 or more. The former president was buried in Grand Rapids, Michigan, where he grew up.

James Earl "Jimmy" Carter, Jr.

39th President of the United States

Term: 1977-1981
Party: Democratic

★★

★ **1924:** James Earl Carter, Jr., was born on October 1 in Plains, Georgia. He was the first U.S. President born in a hospital.

★ **1941:** He graduated from Plains High School and enrolled at Georgia Southwestern College in Americus, Georgia.

★ **1942:** He transferred to the Georgia Institute of Technology in Atlanta.

★ **1943:** Carter fulfilled his life's dream when he was appointed to the U.S. Naval Academy in Annapolis, Maryland.

★ **1946:** He received his naval commission and married Rosalynn Smith of Plains, Georgia, on July 7. The Carters moved to Norfolk, Virginia.

★ **1946-1952:** As a naval officer, Carter and his wife and three young children lived in several states including Virginia, Hawaii, Connecticut, and New York. He served on several battleships and requested a transfer to a submarine fleet. He was admitted to the Navy's new nuclear submarine program and became a senior officer of the *Sea Wolf*, the second U.S. nuclear submarine.

★ **1953:** When his father died, Carter resigned from the Navy and returned with his family to Plains, Georgia, to take over his father's peanut farm business. His mother, a registered nurse, joined the Peace Corps and went to India.

★ **1954-1962:** As a young man living in Plains, Georgia, Jimmy Carter followed in his father's footsteps and began to get involved in the community. He served on several local boards and was appointed to the Sumter County Board of Education.

He began to follow his beliefs and peacefully speak out to promote racial desegregation.

Jimmy Carter

1975: He began actively campaigning for President but was unnoticed as a possible candidate.

1976: In January, he went on a whirlwind campaign and gained recognition. Many voters liked him because he had not served in Washington and was a different breed of politician. He was religious, sincere, and honest.

On November 2, Carter was elected, narrowly defeating Gerald Ford.

1977: He was inaugurated on January 20 in Washington, D.C. His first major decision was to pardon draft evaders of the Vietnam War.

1978: The U.S. established diplomatic relations with the Peoples' Republic of China.

Carter won congressional approval of a national energy program designed to reduce U.S. oil imports.

1962-1966: Carter won a seat in the Georgia State Senate and served two terms.

In 1966, he ran for governor but lost to Lester Maddox.

1967: The Carter's fourth child, Amy, was born.

1971-1975: Carter ran for governor and won the election. He became Georgia's 76th governor on January 12, 1971. As governor, he opened many job opportunities for African Americans in the state government. Because of Georgia state law, he could only serve one term as governor. When he left office, he became more involved in national activities in the Democratic Party and began to set his sights on running for President.

1978: U.S. establishes diplomatic relations with the People's Republic of China.

Carter worked out a peace accord between Egypt and Israel by bringing together the leaders at Camp David in Maryland. This is said to be his greatest success as President.

Two Panama Canal treaties were signed.

★ **1979:** In Iran, revolutionary forces took over the U.S. embassy and seized 52 Americans as hostages.

The Strategic Arms Limitations Treaty (SALT II) between the U.S. and the Soviet Union was signed.

The Soviet Union invaded Afghanistan and U.S.-Soviet relations reached a low point. At Carter's request, the U.S. and many other nations refused to participate in the 1980 summer Olympic Games in Moscow.

Continuing high inflation and gasoline shortages caused Carter's popularity to fall. He requested his entire cabinet to submit their resignations. He made six new appointments hoping to strengthen his administration.

★ **1980:** An armed attempt to rescue the American hostages in Iran failed.

In November Carter was defeated for a second term as President by Ronald Reagan.

★ **1981:** Still President in January, Carter continued to negotiate for the release of the American hostages in Iran. The kidnapping of the U.S. embassy employees was his most difficult problem as President, but he would not give in to terrorist demands. The hostages were released just minutes before he left office. He traveled to Germany to greet them as they returned home.

Carter and his wife returned to Plains, Georgia.

★ **1986:** The Jimmy Carter Library and Museum and The Carter Center of Emory University opened in Atlanta.

★ **1987 to present:** Former President Carter and Rosalynn live in Plains, Georgia. The Jimmy Carter National Historic Site is established there. The Carters volunteer one week every year to work for the Habitat for Humanity.

Carter uses his political experience to promote world peace.

★ **2002:** In October, former President Carter was awarded the Nobel Peace Prize "for his decades of untiring effort to find peaceful solutions to international conflicts, to advance democracy and human rights, and to promote economic and social development." The Norwegian Nobel Committee cited Carter's "vital contribution" to the Camp David Accords between Israel and Egypt.

JIMMY CARTER LIBRARY AND MUSEUM

Ronald Wilson Reagan

40th President of the United States

Term: 1981-1989
Party: Republican

★ **1911:** Ronald Wilson Reagan was born on February 6 in Tampico, Illinois. His nickname was "Dutch."

★ **1928-1932:** He attended Eureka College in Illinois where he studied economics, participated in campus politics and drama, and played on the football team. After graduating he worked as a radio sports announcer in Iowa.

★ **1937:** While in California covering the Chicago Cub's spring training, he got a part as a radio broadcaster in a film for Warner Brothers motion picture studios. This began his 30-year film career. He starred in more than 50 films where he played a variety of roles including western heroes.

★ **1940:** He married actress Jane Wyman.

★ **1942:** During World War II, Reagan joined the Army Air Forces. His nearsighted vision prevented him from serving in combat, but he made training films for the military.

★ **1947:** He became president of the Screen Actors Guild (a trade union for actors) and spent much time working to remove suspected communists from the movie industry. He served through 1952.

★ **1948:** He and Jane Wyman divorced. They had two children, Maureen and Michael. That same year he met his future wife, actress Nancy Davis.

★ **1952:** Reagan married Nancy Davis on March 4.

★ **1954-1962:** He hosted, and sometimes starred in, the weekly television show *General Electric Theater*.

Ronald Reagan

100

TLC10394

THANK YOU, MR. PRESIDENT.

Reagan began the Medi-Cal Program to pay medical bills for the poor.

★ **1962:** Although Reagan had always been a Democrat, he switched and became a Republican.

★ **1964-1965:** Reagan hosted and performed in *Death Valley Days* and made commercials for its sponsor.

He made a powerful campaign speech in support of the Republican candidate for President Barry Goldwater and brought in a record number of contributions. Goldwater lost the election to Lyndon Johnson, but Reagan's strong presentation made him stand out as an exceptional speaker and campaigner for the Republican Party.

★ **1966-1974:** He ran for governor of California and served two terms. He cut the number of people on welfare, began the Medi-Cal program to pay medical bills for the poor, and lowered property taxes. He also doubled the amount of funds to California's public colleges and universities.

★ **1968:** Reagan ran for Republican presidential candidate but lost to Richard Nixon.

★ **1976:** He challenged President Gerald Ford in the presidential election and lost by a slim margin.

★ **1980:** In Reagan's third attempt for the Republican presidential nomination, he won easily. He chose George Herbert Walker Bush as his vice presidential running mate. With high interest rates and high unemployment under President Carter, Reagan won a landslide victory.

★ **1981:** Inaugurated at age 69, he became the oldest President ever elected. He was also the first actor to become President.

When Reagan took office, 52 U.S. hostages held in Iran for 444 days were freed.

On March 30, Reagan was shot by John Hinckley, Jr., while leaving a hotel in Washington, D.C. He was seriously wounded but recovered.

Reagan influenced Congress to cut taxes, social programs, and welfare spending. He also influenced them to spend huge amounts on weapons and the armed forces because he thought Russia might attack the U.S. New radar-evading Stealth bombers and fighters were developed, and new submarines and aircraft carriers were added to the fleet. The U.S. began to develop "Star Wars,"—a space-based missile defense system. This spending policy became known as "Reaganomics." The loss of tax money, combined with greater defense spending, increased the government's debt to the highest it had ever been and took the country into a recession.

Reagan appointed Sandra Day O'Connor as the first woman justice to the Supreme Court.

★ **1983:** The economy started to improve and Reagan was re-elected. He received the largest number of electoral votes in history—525. He was 73 years old and the oldest elected President in history.

⭐ **1984:** Reagan met with the new leader of the Soviet Union Mikhail Gorbachev, and they agreed to destroy some nuclear missiles. This was the first time that the number of nuclear weapons in the world had been reduced.

Reagan had surgery for a cancerous growth and recovered.

His second term was overshadowed by a major policy blunder that almost destroyed his presidency. He had become involved in selling weapons to Iran in order to persuade that country to pressure Islamic militants to release hostages they were holding prisoner in Lebanon. The money made by selling weapons to Iran was used illegally and given to revolutionary forces, the Contras, in Nicaragua.

Shortly after the Democrats regained control of the Senate in the fall of 1986, the sale of weapons and the transfer of money became known. The Democrats organized a full- scale investigation, which became known as the Iran-Contra affair. Reagan's administration was in crisis and several top officials in his administration resigned. Reagan had not been charged with the transfer of funds to the Contras in Nicaragua, but an investigation revealed national security affairs in the White House had been mismanaged.

The Reagan administration was strongly criticized for making foreign policy decisions without notifying Congress. Reagan appeared to have little control over those he appointed. When all the details were released, Reagan's image, reputation, and leadership abilities were badly damaged.

⭐ **1985-1986:** Reagan met with Soviet leader Gorbachev in Geneva, Switzerland. The following year they met in Reykjavik, Iceland. The meetings helped ease tensions.

⭐ **1987:** Reagan and Gorbachev signed a treaty that called for the dismantling of all ground-launched U.S. and Soviet missiles with ranges of 300 to 3400 miles.

⭐ **1989:** Reagan stepped down as President. He and Nancy retired to their ranch, Rancho del Cielo, in Santa Barbara, California. He enjoyed horseback riding, wrote his memoirs and took part in planning his presidential library in nearby Simi Valley.

⭐ **1994:** Reagan announced he had been diagnosed with Alzheimer's disease.

⭐ **2004:** Reagan lived for 10 years after being diagnosed with Alzheimer's disease. He died of pneumonia on June 5th. He lay in state in the Capitol Rotunda. Both the funeral ceremonies in Washington, D.C., and his burial in California were broadcast on national television.

George Herbert Walker Bush

41st President of the United States

Term: 1989-1993
Party: Republican

⭐ **1924:** George Herbert Walker Bush was born on June 12 in Milton, Massachusetts.

⭐ **1942:** After graduating from Phillips Academy in Massachusetts, Bush had planned to go to college. His plans changed when Japan bombed Pearl Harbor in World War II. He joined the Navy and at age 19 became its youngest bomber pilot in the war. He received the Distinguished Flying Cross and three other medals.

⭐ **1945:** Bush had been dating Barbara Pierce since they were teenagers. They married on January 6 after his combat duty was over. The Bushes moved to New Haven, Connecticut, where Bush studied law at Yale University.

⭐ **1948:** Bush graduated from Yale with academic honors and moved to Texas.

⭐ **1953:** With two partners, he set up an oil development company which later merged with another company. Within 10 years, Bush was a successful businessman.

⭐ **1964:** Even with a profitable oil business, Bush wanted to be active in politics. His father had been a U.S. senator from Connecticut. Bush ran for U.S. Congress but was defeated.

⭐ **1966:** He was elected to the House of Representatives and served two terms.

⭐ **1970:** He lost his seat in the House of Representatives.

⭐ **1971:** President Nixon appointed Bush as U.S. ambassador to the United Nations. He held the post for two years.

⭐ **1973:** He became chairman of the Republican National Committee and stood by Nixon during the Watergate scandal. The following year, Bush had the task of delivering a letter to Nixon requesting his resignation.

WHILE PRESIDENT BUSH WAS IN OFFICE, THE COLD WAR CAME TO AN END.

⭐ **1974-1975:** President Ford appointed Bush as chief of the U.S. Liaison Office to the People's Republic of China. Bush was the first U.S. representative to receive a post in Communist China.

⭐ **1976-1977:** Upon his return from China, Ford appointed Bush director of the Central Intelligence Agency (CIA). He had been given positions of great responsibility and had progressed steadily in the U.S. government and in the Republican Party.

⭐ **1980:** Bush lost the Republican presidential nomination to Ronald Reagan. Reagan then chose Bush as his vice presidential running mate. Reagan won the election and Bush became Vice President.

⭐ **1981-1989:** He served as Vice President for eight years and gained a lot of experience.

In July 1985, Bush served as acting President for about eight hours while President Reagan had surgery.

⭐ **1989:** When Reagan's two terms of office were up, Bush ran for President and won against Democrat Michael Dukakis.

He took office at age 64.

The Cold War between the U.S. and Russia came to an end. Communist governments in Eastern Europe ended and the Berlin Wall dividing East and West Germany came down.

Bush invaded Panama to seize its dictator Manuel Noriega for drug trafficking.

⭐ **1990:** East and West Germany became one united country.

TLC10394

When Iraq invaded the small neighboring country of Kuwait, the U.S. and 29 other countries sent troops to Kuwait to protect and recapture the country. This was done after Bush obtained a U.N. resolution approving the use of force against Iraq and its dictator, Saddam Hussein.

Although he had promised not to raise taxes when he was campaigning for President, he broke his promise and increased various taxes. Unemployment increased and the economy slowed. Many Americans felt the U.S. was losing much business to Japan.

⭐ **1991:** The U.S. and air forces from other countries began a quick and successful military campaign against Iraq. It started with the bombing of Baghdad, the capital of Iraq, on January 17. One month later, on February 24, a land invasion began. Within four days Iraq had been defeated and Kuwait was free. Saddam Hussein, however, remained in power. This was known as the

Gulf War. Bush's popularity soared.

The Soviet Union was transformed into the Commonwealth of Independent States.

Bush's popularity fell 30 percent because of a slow economy, a high national debt, cutbacks in popular social programs, and for breaking his promise about no new taxes.

⭐ **1992:** Bush ran for re-election but was defeated by Arkansas governor Bill Clinton.

⭐ **1993:** He left office and retired, dividing his time between the Bushes' homes in Houston, Texas, and Kennebunkport, Maine.

1991: THE SOVIET UNION WAS TRANSFORMED INTO THE COMMONWEALTH OF INDEPENDENT STATES.

William Jefferson "Bill" Clinton

42ⁿᵈ President of the United States

Term: 1993-2001
Party: Democratic

★★★★★★★★★★★★★★★★★★★★★★★★★★★★★★★★★★★★★★★

★ **1946:** William (Bill) Clinton was born on August 19 in Hope, Arkansas. His father died three months before he was born, and he was given his father's exact name, William Jefferson Blythe. When his mother remarried a few years later, William was given his stepfather's last name, Clinton.

★ **1963:** From the age of nine, Clinton showed an interest in politics and became active in student government. When he was 17, he was selected as a delegate to the American Legion Boys Nation Leadership Camp to go on a trip to Washington, D.C. He was part of a group that was invited to the White House. He met and shook hands with his idol, President John F. Kennedy. This experience made such an impression on Clinton that he decided he wanted to enter politics.

★ **1968:** Clinton graduated from Georgetown University in Washington, D.C. That year he won a two-year Rhodes scholarship and went to study at Oxford University in England. After he left Oxford, he won a scholarship to Yale Law School.

★ **1970-1972:** He took some time off from law school to work for the presidential campaign of Democratic Senator George McGovern of South Dakota.

★ **1973:** He received a law degree from Yale University in New Haven, Connecticut. At Yale he met his future wife, Hillary Rodham, who was also studying law. After graduating from Yale, he returned to Arkansas, where he served for a short period as a staff lawyer for the U.S. House of Representatives Judiciary Committee.

Bill Clinton

TLC10394

Hillary Clinton

★ **1992:** Clinton became the Democratic candidate for President and campaigned against incumbent President George Herbert Walker Bush. Ross Perot of Texas also ran, making it a three-candidate race. Clinton won the election.

As President, he appointed more women and minorities to cabinet positions than any former President.

Hillary Clinton became a very involved First Lady. She attempted to reform the national health care system and provide better health care for all Americans, but her plan was defeated by Congress. She also worked to improve the welfare of single mothers and their children. She became the most influential first lady since Eleanor Roosevelt.

★ **1974:** Clinton unsuccessfully campaigned for a seat in the U.S. House of Representatives. He taught at the University of Arkansas Law School and became active in Arkansas Democratic politics.

★ **1975:** Bill and Hillary were married on October 11.

★ **1976:** He was elected State's Attorney in Arkansas.

★ **1978-1992:** In 1978, Clinton was elected governor of Arkansas. At 32, he was the youngest governor in the nation. In the next election, he was defeated. Not one to give up, he ran for governor again, regained the office, and was the governor of Arkansas for 10 years. During this time, he was elected president of the National Governors Association and was voted by his fellow governors as the nation's most successful governor.

In 1991, he announced he would be a candidate for President of the United States.

THANK YOU, MRS. CLINTON!

HILLARY CLINTON WORKED TO IMPROVE THE WELFARE OF SINGLE MOTHERS AND THEIR CHILDREN. 1992

★ **1993:** Clinton was successful in achieving one of his major foreign policy goals when Congress approved the North American Free Trade Agreement (NAFTA). This ended trade restrictions between the U.S., Mexico, and Canada.

★ **1996:** Clinton concentrated on rebuilding the U.S. economy, and at the end of his first term, the country's economy was the best it had been in many years. He was easily re-elected.

★ **1998:** In the middle of his second term, Clinton faced very serious charges. The House of Representatives brought charges of impeachment against him. He was the first President to face impeachment since Andrew Johnson in 1868. Clinton was charged with lying under oath and obstructing justice for not telling important information about a relationship with a White House intern.

★ **1999:** After a trial by the U.S. Senate, Clinton was found to be innocent of all charges and was not impeached. With the effects of the impeachment and a scandal hanging over the rest of his term, he continued as a controversial President.

★ **2000:** Clinton ended his two terms as a controversial yet popular President. The United States was richer than it had ever been in its history.

TLC10394

George W. Bush

43rd President of the United States

Term: 2001- 2009
Party: Republican

★★

★ **1946:** George Walker Bush was born on July 6, in New Haven, Connecticut. His father, George Herbert Walker Bush, was the 41st President of the United States.

Bush grew up in Midland and Houston, Texas.

★ **1961:** At age 15, he was sent to Phillips Academy in Andover, Massachusetts, where his father had gone to school.

★ **1964-1968:** He attended Yale University in Connecticut where he studied history.

★ **1968-1973:** After graduation, Bush enlisted in the Texas National Guard. He was in flight training as a second lieutenant for two years as an F-102 pilot. This was the time of the Vietnam War. After two years of training, he served part-time for three and a half years.

★ **1973-1975:** He entered Harvard Business School in Cambridge, Massachusetts. He graduated with a Masters in Business Administration.

★ **1975-1986:** After graduating, he returned to Texas and began his career in the oil and gas business. He worked in the energy industry until 1986.

★ 1977: Bush married Laura Welch on November 5. She was a teacher and librarian.

★ 1981: President Bush and his wife Laura have fraternal twin daughters. Barbara was the first born and was named after her grandmother Barbara Bush. Jenna was named after her maternal grandmother Jenna Welch.

★ 1988-1989: After working on his father's successful presidential campaign, Bush and a group of partners bought the Texas Rangers baseball team. Willie Mays had always been Bush's hero.

★ 1989-1994: As a business partner, Bush managed the Texas Rangers until he was elected governor of Texas in November 1994.

★ 1995: He served as governor of Texas from January 1995 until December 21, 2000.

★ 2000: Bush was nominated as the Republican presidential nominee. His vice presidential running mate was Richard (Dick) Cheney.

The presidential election was one of the most unusual in history. The election was a very close one, and Florida's votes ended up determining the winner. The number of votes in Florida for Bush and his Democratic opponent Al Gore was so close they had to be recounted. The final number of votes was very controversial and both Bush and Gore went to court to try to win Florida's votes.

The fight went to the U.S. Supreme Court, and the justices selected George W. Bush as President. The election divided the American people. Many thought the Supreme Court did not have the right to determine the President.

★ 2001: Bush was inaugurated on January 20.

On September 11, 19 terrorists took over the control of four American passenger airplanes. Two crashed into the World Trade Center towers in New York City. Another crashed into the Pentagon in Washington, D.C. The fourth plane crashed in a field in Pennsylvania when passengers tried to stop the terrorists. More than 3000 people, most of them Americans, were killed that day.

September 11 began the U.S. war on terrorism, and it became Bush's main

concern as President. The government created a new Department of Homeland Security to protect the American people.

As part of Bush's "War on Terror," U.S. troops invaded Afghanistan to overthrow the Taliban government.

★ **2002:** Another major concern for Bush was the threat of weapons of mass destruction in Iraq. He threatened war against Iraq unless its leader, Saddam Hussein, allowed U.S. forces to inspect the country to determine if there were such weapons.

The economy had been very high when former President Bill Clinton was in office. When Bush took office, the economy dropped to the lowest level it had been for a long time. Many Americans felt Bush was ignoring the economy and focusing only on the war on terrorism and the crisis in Iraq.

★ **2003:** Although the United Nations Security Council voted against invading Iraq, President Bush—along with Great Britain as the only major ally—began to invade Iraq on March 19. The coalition forces of the U.S. and Great Britain destroyed major cities, and many Iraqi soldiers and civilians surrendered.

One month after invading Iraq, plans were underway to begin rebuilding destroyed cities and towns. There was realistic hope that the Iraqi people would begin to create a democratic government and no longer be forced to live under the rule of dictator Saddam Hussein.

The U.S. invaded Iraq in order to overthrow the dictator Saddam Hussein. After only a few weeks of fighting, the U.S. controlled the country. The alleged reason for the invasion was the belief that Iraq had weapons of mass destruction. Later, that belief was proven to be untrue.

★ **2004:** Photographs came to light showing U.S. soldiers abusing Iraqis at the Abu Graib prison. This caused a big scandal in the United States.

The 9/11 Commission said that, in spite of what the Bush administration had believed, there was no connection between Iraq and the terrorists who destroyed the World Trade Center.

Bush was re-elected President in November.

★ **2005:** Hurricane Katrina virtually destroyed New Orleans when the levees broke and water flooded the city. The number killed reached 1,833 people.

★ **2006:** Former Vice President Al Gore released the movie "An Inconvenient Truth," which warned about global warming. Many people became more concerned about the planet's environment.

The Democrats regained control of the House and the Senate.

★ **2007:** Rebels were still fighting against U.S. forces in Iraq. To end this rebellion, President Bush authorized a "surge" of 20,000 more troops to that country.

★ **2008:** The United States suffered an economic downturn due in part to fraudulent home mortgages and the rapid rise in the price of gasoline.

Barack Hussein Obama

44ⁿᵈ President of the United States

Term: 2009-
Party: Democratic

★ **1961:** Barack Hussein Obama, Jr., was born in Honolulu, Hawaii, on August 4th. His father, Barack Hussein Obama, Sr., was from Kenya, Africa. His mother, Ann Dunham, was from the Midwestern United States.

★ **1963:** Barack Obama, Sr., returned to Kenya, leaving his family in Hawaii. Barack and Anne's marriage ended.

★ **1967:** Ann met and married Lolo Soetoro. The whole family moved to Indonesia.

★ **1971-1979:** Barack, Jr., moved back to Hawaii and lived with his grandparents while he attended the Punahou School. His half-sister Maya was born.

★ **1979:** Barack, Jr., graduated from Punahou School. He received a full scholarship from Occidental College in Los Angeles.

★ **1981-1983:** He transferred to Columbia University in New York City. He graduated and was employed at Business International Corporation in NYC.

★ **1984:** Barack moved to Chicago to work as a community organizer.

★ **1988:** Barack began studying at Harvard Law School.

★ **1989:** He worked at a law firm during the summer and there met his future wife Michelle Robinson.

★ **1990-1991:** Barack was the first African American to be elected President of the Harvard Law review.

★ **1991:** Obama graduated from Harvard Law School and worked at a law office in Chicago.

★ **1992:** He became the executive director of Project Vote in Illinois. The same year he married Michelle Robinson. Obama began teaching at the University of Chicago Law School.

★ **1997-2004:** Obama served as a state senator in the Illinois legislature.

★ **2000:** Barack wanted to run as the Democratic candidate for a seat in the U.S. House of Representatives, but he lost in the primary election.

★ **2004:** Barack delivered the keynote address at the Democratic National Convention in Boston. The speech was a great success.

★ **2005:** Obama began serving as a U.S. Senator from Illinois.

★ **2007:** On February 10th, Obama announced that he was running for the Democratic nomination for President of the United States.

★ **2008:** On November 4th, Obama became the first African American to be elected President of the United States.

TLC10394